MERCURY READER

a custom publication

Reading and Writing Literacies

Collin Craig
Nancy C. DeJoy
Steven T. Lessner

Pearson Learning Solutions

New York   Boston   San Francisco
London   Toronto   Sydney   Tokyo   Singapore   Madrid
Mexico City   Munich   Paris   Cape Town   Hong Kong   Montreal

Senior Vice President, Editorial and Marketing: Patrick F. Boles
Senior Sponsoring Editor: Natalie Danner
Development Editor: Mary Kate Paris
Assistant Editor: Jill Johnson
Operations Manager: Eric M. Kenney
Production Manager: Jennifer Berry
Rights Manager: Jillian Santos
Art Director: Renée Sartell
Cover Designers: Kristen Kiley, Blythe Russo, Tess Mattern, and Renée Sartell

Cover Art: "Gigantia Mountains & Sea of Cortes," by R.G.K. Photography, Copyright © Tony Stone Images; "Dime," courtesy of the Shaw Collection; "Open Book On Table Edge w/Pencil," courtesy of PhotoAlto Photography/Veer Incorporated; "Open Book On Table Near Table's Corner," courtesy of Fancy Photography/Veer Incorporated; "Scrabble Pieces and a Die," by G. Herbst, courtesy of PlainPicture Photography/Veer Incorporated; "Binary codes in bowls," by John Still, courtesy of Photographer's Choice/Getty Images; "Close-up of an open book," courtesy of Glowimages/Getty Images; "College Students Sitting At Tables," courtesy of Blend/PunchStock; "Red and blue circles," courtesy of Corbis Images; "Laptop screen showing photograph of landscape," courtesy of Martin Holtcamp/Getty Images; "Apples flying," courtesy of Arne Morgenstern/Getty Images.

Please visit our website at *www.pearsoncustom.com.*

Attention bookstores: For permission to return any unsold stock, contact us at *pe-uscustomreturns@pearson.com.*

Pearson Learning Solutions, 501 Boylston Street, Suite 900, Boston, MA 02116
A Pearson Education Company
www.pearsoned.com

ISBN 10: 0-558-63351-X
ISBN 13: 978-0-558-63351-6

Contents

Revising Literacies

Appendix I: Paper Assignments

Electronic Readings
These readings are available online

Lived Literacies
The Screenwriter's Tale by Jennifer Lawler

Cultural Literacies
Football Red and Baseball Green: The Heroics and
 Bucolics of American Sport by Murray Ross

Disciplinary Literacies
One Carpenter's Life by Larry Haun
Learning to Read Biology: One Student's Rhetorical
 Development in College by Christina Haas
Writing Information Literacy in the Classroom:
 Pedagogical Elements and Implications
The Nature of Reading and Writing at Work by
 William Diehl and Larry Mikulecky

Remixing/Technological Literacies
Teaching Visual Literacy in a Multimodal Age by
 Glenda Rakes
For Some, The Blogging Never Stops
 You, The DJ by Sasha Frere-Jones
Popular Music in School: Remixing the Issues by
 Robert H. Woody

Revising Literacies
Literacy in Three Metaphors by Sylvia Scribner
Stories, Not Information: Transforming Information
 Literacy by Jeff Purdue
Being an Ally by Helen Fox
The Noble Lecture by Toni Morrison

INTRODUCTION

When making decisions about what texts to include in this Reader we had long conversations about what we have learned from our first-year writing students over the past few years. We wanted to make selections that we knew would help students make successful transitions to writing, reading, and researching in higher education in America. (We also forced ourselves to limit selections so that teachers and students can add additional texts appropriate for their particular contexts.) Some of the Readings included here have worked well in the past, others are new readings that we selected because they open spaces for students to make valuable contributions to our understanding of literacy in the contexts of their lives. Each of the readings included here, then, opens up conversations about literacy that invite students to make the conceptual shift from thinking of themselves as consumers of knowledge to understanding themselves as participants who make important contributions to their communities. Sometimes, those contributions change the way we think, other times they may also change practices (like the student project that inspired one teacher to include undergraduate students in her professional presentations). Our students tell us that the transition away from education as the consumption of knowledge (and tests that measure the quality of your consumption) and toward education as a participatory activity that sets expectations for new contributions is challenging, exciting, uneven, frustrating, and rewarding—usually all at once!

We know that these challenges and opportunities occur because as students adjust to life in higher education and choose their major, they are introduced to multiple conventions of knowledge-making that will require them to think about language and learning in different ways. As a way of helping teachers and learners focus on these new challenges and opportunities we chose readings that demonstrate an understanding of literacy as a broad and flexible concept that can help us understand ourselves, one another, and our worlds in engaged—and engaging—ways. From our own experiences we know that we live in evolving cultures that constantly shape how we "read" and, function in, the world. Our selections of readings demonstrate how diverse communities gain access to and use multiple literacies for multiple aims. We hope that our decision to organize around the themes of personal, cultural, disciplinary, technological, and revisionary forms of literacy inspires teachers and students to contribute their own stories, ideas, critical analyses, and suggestions for how we might all work to use language to improve our own lives and the lives of all of the members of the diverse communities to which we belong. We hope that taken collectively, the readings in this book encourage writing and researching that helps us all see our own and one anothers' potential for successful, meaningful lives as literate people in higher education and beyond.

We aimed to create a reading experience that was relevant to each of the types of literacy we use to organize the sections of this book. But we also selected readings that can be used across sections as students and teachers work together throughout the semester. For example, Elizabeth Wong's "The Struggle to Be an All American Girl" demonstrates lived experiences with learning English as a Chinese student; but she also revises her values about American culture when she is faced with learning how to merge her American and Chinese identities. Sylvia Scribmer's "Literacy in Three Metaphors" revises some major assumptions about literacy as merely reading and writing; but it does so in a way that meets the expectations for writing in her discipline. Similarly, the videos from TED.com that are listed at the end of each section are appropriate for use with the essays in that section. However, they can also be used in combination with readings from other sections. Shereen El Feki's talk "Culture in the Arab World" is listed in the Remixing/Technological section, but it could also be used as you explore Cultural Literacies. We group readings and other resources thematically because we want our readers to be able to see consistencies and differences across literacy themes. We encourage you to rearrange them as you go because we want you to create your own connections across writing assignments.

We invite you to think about the types of writing and researching that you can generate with this Reader and encourage you to contemplate how you might participate in conversations that are situated in multiple contexts. As you use this Reader think about what you might add to these conversations. For example:

- How does your own literacy history lead to suggestions about how to enhance other students' transitions to higher education?
- What are language practices that are crucial in your everyday life?
- How do some of the literacy artifacts in your life indicate a larger set of values?
- What are the writing, reading, and researching practices most common in fields connected to your major, and how might you create a literacy plan that prepares you to be successful?
- How do technologies enhance and/or inhibit forms of literacy not usually studied in school, but vital to our happiness outside of school?
- How might you use inquiry into literacy as a strategy toward developing new knowledge and revising existing ideas?
- How might you use that inquiry to enter multiple conversations?

We know that these are big questions. But we also know that asking them together will result in richer relationships, better conversations, and more effective responses to our worlds than we could ever create alone.

Lived Literacies

Lived Literacies: Introduction

The readings in this section invite you to explore the ways that literacy and the values and practices associated with literacy affect our lived experiences of self, other and world. They should help you to get some ideas about how specific literacy practices, attitudes, etc. affect particular parts of people's experiences of self, other and world. As you read, pay attention to the invention strategies used by the writers. For example, in "Mother Tongue," Amy Tan reflects on her experiences by creating a contrast between how she uses language with and for her mother and how she uses language in her life as a writer and presenter. Reflecting by exploring a contrast is an invention strategy you might use to explore your own literacy history. In "The Screenwriter's Tale," Jennifer Lawler observes the ways that people react to her life as a writer who does not stick to academic writing even though she is an academic. Observing people's reaction to her difference is an invention strategy that helps Lawler understand and communicate these reactions and to explore what they mean in the specific context of her department. You might want to use observation as an invention strategy as you explore possible focuses for your own literacy narrative. Don't worry about finding all of the invention strategies or worrying about if the ones you see are the 'right' ones. At this point, just concentrate on reading as part of the writing process, a part that can help you discover new ways to go about generating ideas and trying new invention strategies.

Welcome to St. Paul's
Lorene Cary

Lorene Cary studied in England after graduating from the University of Pennsylvania (M. A., 1978). She has worked for Time *and* TV Guide *and taught at and served as a member of the Board of Trustees of St. Paul's, an exclusive boarding school she attended. This essay describes her arrival at St. Paul's, which until a few years earlier had been all-white and all-male. Excerpted from* Black Ice *(1991), a story about her experiences at St. Paul's, the essay reveals the many life changes she encountered as an African-American girl in a very different, almost all-white, almost all-male world.*

My family and I stood in the Rectory just a year and a half after Lee's first tea. Unlike her, I was armed with the experience of a proper, on-campus interview, and I was escorted by attractive young parents and a cuddly kid sister. Unlike Ed Shockley, I was not afraid that the white boys were going to catch me alone in the woods one night and beat me up. But for the first time, I had a whiff, as subtle as the scent of the old books that lined the wall, of my utter aloneness in this new world. I reached into myself for the head-to-the-side, hands-on-hips cockiness that had brought me here and found just enough of it to keep me going.

My dormitory was around the corner from the Rectory, over a bridge and across the road from the library. Inside, just off the common room, steps led to the open doorway of the housemaster. He, too, was on hand to greet us.

I wasn't sure about Mr. Hawley. He had a round face whose top half was nearly bald and whose bottom half was covered with a full, tweed-colored beard. Between the top and bottom halves a pair of

From *Black Ice* by Lorene Cary. Published by Alfred A. Knopf, Inc. Copyright © 1991 by Lorene Cary.

glasses perched on a small nose and caught the light. He made a funny face when he spied my sister: "And look what you brought along! We've got a couple of those creatures running around somewhere. I'll see if they've been run over yet by some station wagon gone berserk."

I was later to learn that all the intelligence and will, all the imagination and mischief in that face was revealed in the pale eyes behind the glasses, but on this first meeting, I could only bring myself to concentrate on the beard and the Kriss Kringle month.

5 Mr. Hawley, it turned out, had family in Philadelphia, so we talked about the city, and my parents described for him just exactly where we lived.

Like other St. Paul's buildings, the Hawleys' house had alcoves, staircases, and a courtyard, that presented to me a facade of impenetrable, almost European, privacy. The housemaster's home was directly accessible from the dormitory, but only by going from the vestibule into the common room, then up stairs, through a heavy wooden door, into a hallway, and another, inner door. Once in the living room, I could see through the windows that we were across the street from the gray granite library, but I would not have known it had the drapes been pulled. The architecture that I so admired from the outside did not yield itself up to me from within as I had expected. I now felt disconcerted, as I had in the Rectory. Mr. Hawley wanted to know just how far one would drive along Baltimore Pike to get to Yeadon, and I, standing in his living room, had no idea where his kitchen might be.

Mrs. Hawley, a short, soft-spoken woman, appeared from the rear hallway. Like her husband, she said ironic things, but more gently. Startlingly blond children came with her, one peeking from behind her skirt.

Mr. Hawley directed us to my room and showed my father where to park by the back door so that we could unload more handily. We carried my things up from a basement entrance. Doors whooshed open and closed as other girls and their families came and went, and the halls echoed with the sounds of mothers' heels.

My room faced east. In the afternoon it seemed dull and empty and dark.

10 "This'll be lovely when you get it all fixed up," my mother said, by which I assumed that it looked dull to her, too.

Fine dust had settled contentedly over the sturdy oak bureau and cloudy mirror, over the charming, squat little oak desk and chair and in the corners of the closet. White people, as we said, were not personally fastidious (any black woman who'd ever been a maid could tell you that, and some did, in appalling detail, so I'd heard stories). I was determined to give the place a good wash.

The casement windows matched those elsewhere on campus. My father opened one, tightened the wing nut to hold the sash in place, and stood looking out into the meadow. Then he peeked into the room next door, which was still empty, and recalled how, at Lincoln University, the first students to arrive scavenged the best furniture in the dormitory. "If there's any furniture you don't like, better speak now," he joked. "I guess you wouldn't want to do that here."

I checked the room next door, and pronounced, with laughter but not conviction, that I'd gotten a fair bargain.

The room seemed crowded with all of us about. I found myself chattering on, very gaily, about where I would put my things. What with the windows at one end, the narrow bed against one wall, the bureau, the desk, the radiator, the closet, the door leading into the next room, the door leading in, and the economy of my possessions, there were few options, realistically, for interior design.

15   Still, I could not stop buzzing. So long as we stood crowded to-   15
gether in the room, my sister jumping on the naked mattress, my mother wondering about smoking a cigarette, my father by the open window clenching his jaw and rubbing the back of his neck, and me burbling and babbling as if words were British soldiers marching in pointless columns, bright and gay, with flags and bright brass buttons on crimson-colored breasts, on and on and on into battle; so long as we had nothing to do except to wait for the next thing to do; so long as the intolerable closeness remained and the intolerable separation loomed to be made, so long would this adrenaline rush through me, anarchic, atavistic, compelling.

Outside the move-in continued. Convinced that I was missing yet another ritual of initiation, I ran down the hall to check the bulletin board. As I stood reading, an Asian boy propelled himself into the vestibule. He introduced himself without smiling and asked me my name. Then, addressing me by the name I gave, he asked whether or not I lived in Simpson House.

"Listen," he said. "There's a girl upstairs. She's just moved in. Her name is Fumiko, and she's from Japan. She can hardly speak any English at all. She understands a lot, but she really needs someone to go and make her feel welcome."

"Do you speak Japanese?"

"Of course not." (He was Chinese-American.) He appeared to be reevaluating me. "Look, is anyone else around?"

20 "I don't know. I've just arrived myself." 20

"Well, welcome! Look, we've been helping her, but she needs a girl in her own house, and guys can't come in. Maybe you can tell some of the other girls. Really, she's only just come to the country."

Reluctantly, I agreed. I went to the room on the second floor that the boy had described, and found her. I introduced myself. We tried hard to pronounce each other's names, and we laughed at our mistakes. Fumiko was taller than I. She kept suppressing bows. We agreed to meet again later.

I returned to my family much calmer than I'd left, and I told them about my new friend. Now my mother seemed agitated. Just before we left for dinner, she began to tell me what items of clothing should go into which drawer.

"You always put underwear in the top. See, it's the shallowest one. Big, bulky things like sweaters and jeans go down at the bottom. But, now, please don't just jam your things in. I don't want you walking around here with stuff that's all jerked up."

25 "I know where things go." 25

"Listen. Skirts, your good pants, all that staff needs to be hung up. Let's see how this is packed." My mother unzipped one of the suitcases on the bed. "You know, maybe you might want us to take this big one home. I can't see where you have room to store it."

I watched my mother lift layers of underwear delicately from their berths. Her hands, precise, familiar, called up in me a frenzy of possession. "I've got all night to unpack," I said. "Please don't. I should do that."

"I'll just help you get started. Lord, I hope you don't start putting together any of those crazy outfits you concoct at home. I know you think that stuff looks cute, but it doesn't. You didn't pack any of those fishnet stockings, I hope." Mama selected a drawer for panties and one for bras and slips. I'd brought a girdle—hers, of course—that was hidden in the next layer.

9

"I *really* want to do that myself."

30 "I'm not taking anything away from you." Her voice rose with 30 maternal indignation.

"Let the child do it herself," my father said.

I knew that they were going to fight. It would be a silent fight, because we were, even in this room, in public, so long as we were on school grounds. I did not see how we would avoid it. We'd been cooped up together, as my parents called it, all day.

Then my mother laughed. "All right, all right, I was just getting you started," she said. "You'd think I was doing something wrong."

We left for dinner, and I closed my door.

Reading Ourselves and the World Around Us*

Alberto Manguel

Alberto Manguel (1948–) was born in Buenos Aires, reared in Israel, and, in 1981, was granted Canadian citizenship. His has edited anthologies of fantasy literature, short fiction by Latin American women, erotica, and ghost and mystery stories. He has also written a novel, News from a Foreign Country Game *(1991) and a nonfiction work,* A History of Reading *(1996), from which the following essay comes. In this brief excerpt, Manguel describes an early memory of literacy, the moment at which he realized that he could read.*

1   I first discovered that I could read at the age of four. I had seen, over and over again, the letters that I knew (because I had been told) were the names of the pictures under which they sat. The boy drawn in thick black lines, dressed in red shorts and a green shirt (that same red and green cloth from which all the other images in the book were cut, dogs and cats and trees and thin tall mothers), was also somehow, I realized, the stern black shapes beneath him, as if the boy's body had been dismembered into three clean-cut figures: one arm and the torso, **b**; the severed head so perfectly round, **o**; and the limp, low-hanging legs, **y**. I drew eyes in the round face, and a smile, and filled in the hollow circle of the torso. But there was more: I knew that not only did these shapes mirror the boy above them, but they also could tell me precisely what the boy was doing, arms stretched out and legs apart. **The boy runs**, said the shapes. He wasn't jumping, as I might

*Editor's title

have thought, or pretending to be frozen into place, or playing a game whose rules and purpose were unknown to me. **The boy runs**.

And yet these realizations were common acts of conjuring, less interesting because someone else had performed them for me. Another reader—my nurse, probably—had explained the shapes and now, every time the pages opened to the image of this exuberant boy, I knew what the shapes beneath him meant. There was pleasure in this, but it wore thin. There was no surprise.

Then one day, from the window of a car (the destination of that journey is now forgotten), I saw a billboard by the side of the road. The sight could not have lasted very long; perhaps the car stopped for a moment, perhaps it just slowed down long enough for me to see, large and looming, shapes similar to those in my book, but shapes that I had never seen before. And yet, all of a sudden, I knew what they were; I heard them in my head, they metamorphosed from black lines and white spaces into a solid, sonorous, meaningful reality. I had done this all by myself. No one had performed the magic for me. I and the shapes were alone together, revealing ourselves in a silently respectful dialogue. Since I could turn bare lines into living reality, I was all-powerful. I could read.

What that word was on the long-past billboard I no longer know (vaguely I seem to remember a word with several As in it), but the impression of suddenly being able to comprehend what before I could only gaze at is as vivid today as it must have been then. It was like acquiring an entirely new sense, so that now certain things no longer consisted merely of what my eyes could see, my ears could hear, my tongue could taste, my nose could smell, my fingers could feel, but of what my whole body could decipher, translate, give voice to, read.

The readers of books, into whose family I was unknowingly entering (we always think that we are alone in each discovery, and that every experience, from death to birth, is terrifyingly unique), extend or concentrate a function common to us all. Reading letters on a page is only one of its many guises. The astronomer reading a map of stars that no longer exist; the Japanese architect reading the land on which a house is to be built so as to guard it from evil forces; the zoologist reading the spoor of animals in the forest; the card-player reading her partner's gestures before playing the winning card; the dancer reading the choreographer's notations, and the public reading the dancer's movements on the stage; the weaver reading the intricate design of a carpet being woven; the organ-player reading various simultaneous strands of music orchestrated on the page: the parent reading the baby's face for signs of joy or fright, or wonder; the Chinese fortune-teller reading the ancient marks on the shell of a tortoise; the lover blindly reading the loved one's body at night, under the sheets; the psychiatrist helping patients read their own bewildering dreams; the Hawaiian fisherman reading the ocean currents by plunging a hand into the water, the farmer reading the weather in the sky—all these share with bookreaders the craft of deciphering and translating signs. Some of these readings are coloured by the knowledge that the thing read was created for this specific purpose by other human beings—music notation or road signs, for instance—or by the gods—the tortoise shell, the sky at night. Others belong to chance.

And yet, in every case, it is the reader who reads the sense; it is the reader who grants or recognizes in an object, place or event a certain possible readability; it is the reader who must attribute meaning to a system of signs, and then decipher it. We all read ourselves and the world around us in order to glimpse what and where we are. We read to understand, or to begin to understand. We cannot do but read. Reading, almost as much as breathing, is our essential function.

Growing Up

Russell Baker

*Russell Baker (1925–) was born in a rural town in Vir-
ginia and grew up in New Jersey and Maryland. He received his B. A. in English from Johns Hopkins University
in 1947 and worked as a reporter for the* Baltimore Sun
and then the New York Times. *In 1962 he began writing
his "Observer" column for the* Times, *which was syndicated in over 400 newspapers for more than two decades.
His topics range from the mundane everyday annoyances to
serious social problems, and his style is generally casual but
thoughtful. In 1979 he received the Pulitzer Prize for distinguished commentary; he received the Prize again for his
autobiography* Growing Up *(1982), from which the following selection is excerpted. His collections of columns and
essays include* All Things Considered *(1965),* Poor Russell's Almanac *(1972),* So This Is Depravity *(1980)* The
Rescue of Miss Yaskell and Other Pipe Dreams *(1983),
and* There's a Country in My Cellar *(1990). The following excerpt from his autobiography describes, with humor
and insight, the moment when he decides he wants to become a writer.*

1   I began working in journalism when I was eight years old. It was
my mother's idea. She wanted me to "make something" of myself
and, after a levelheaded appraisal of my strengths, decided I had
better start young if I was to have any chance of keeping up with the
competition.

The flaw in my character which she had already spotted was lack
of "gumption." My idea of a perfect afternoon was lying in front of
the radio rereading my favorite Big Little Book, *Dick Tracy Meets*

Stooge Viller. My mother despised inactivity. Seeing me having a good time in repose, she was powerless to hide her disgust. "You've got no more gumption than a bump on a log," she said. "Get out in the kitchen and help Doris do those dirty dishes."

My sister Doris, though two years younger than I, had enough gumption for a dozen people. She positively enjoyed washing dishes, making beds, and cleaning the house. When she was only seven she could carry a piece of short-weighted cheese back to the A&P, threaten the manager with legal action, and come back triumphantly with the full quarter-pound we'd paid for and a few ounces extra thrown in for forgiveness. Doris could have made something of herself if she hadn't been a girl. Because of this defect, however, the best she could hope for was a career as a nurse or schoolteacher, the only work that capable females were considered up to. in those days.

This must have saddened my mother, this twist of fate that had allocated all the gumption to the daughter and left her with a son who was content with Dick Tracy and Stooge Viller. If disappointed, though, she wasted no energy on self-pity. She would make me make something of myself whether I wanted to or not. "The Lord helps those who help themselves," she said. That was the way her mind worked.

5 She was realistic about the difficulty. Having sized up the material the Lord had given her to mold, she didn't overestimate what she could do with it. She didn't insist that I grow up to be President of the United States.

Fifty years ago parents still asked boys if they wanted to grow up to be President, and asked it not jokingly but seriously. Many parents who were hardly more than paupers still believed their sons could do it. Abraham Lincoln had done it. We were only sixty-five years from Lincoln. Many a grandfather who walked among us could remember Lincoln's time. Men of grandfatherly age were the worst for asking if you wanted to grow up to be President. A surprising number of little boys said yes and meant it.

I was asked many times myself. No, I would say, I didn't want to grow up to be President. My mother was present during one of these interrogations. An elderly uncle, having posed the usual question and exposed my lack of interest in the Presidency, asked, "Well, what *do* you want to be when you grow up?"

I loved to pick through trash piles and collect empty bottles, tin cans with pretty labels, and discarded magazines. The most desirable job on earth sprang instantly to mind. "I want to be a garbage man," I said.

My uncle smiled, but my mother had seen the first distressing evidence of a bump budding on a log. "Have a little gumption, Russell," she said. Her calling me Russell was a signal of unhappiness. When she approved of me I was always "Buddy."

When I turned eight years old she decided that the job of starting me on the road toward making something of myself could no longer be safely delayed. "Buddy," she said one day, "I want you to come home right after school this afternoon. Somebody's coming and I want you to meet him."

When I burst in that afternoon she was in conference in the parlor with an executive of the Curtis Publishing Company. She introduced me. He bent low from the waist and shook my hand. Was it true as my mother had told him, he asked, that I longed for the opportunity to conquer the world of business?

My mother replied that I was blessed with a rare determination to make something of myself.

"That's right," I whispered.

"But have you got the grit, the character, the never-say-quit spirit it takes to succeed in business?"

My mother said I certainly did.

"That's right," I said.

He eyed me silently for a long pause, as though weighing whether I could be trusted to keep his confidence, then spoke man-to-man. Before taking a crucial step, he said, he wanted to advise me that working for the Curtis Publishing Company placed enormous responsibility on a young man. It was one of the great companies of America. Perhaps the greatest publishing house in the world. I had heard, no doubt, of the *Saturday Evening Post?*

Heard of it? My mother said that everyone in our house had heard of the *Saturday Post* and that I, in fact, read it with religious devotion.

Then doubtless he said, we were also familiar with those two monthly pillars of the magazine world, the *Ladies Home Journal* and the *Country Gentleman.*

Indeed we were familiar with them, said my mother.

Representing the *Saturday Evening Post* was one of the weightiest honors that could be bestowed in the world of business, he said. He was personally proud of being a part of that great corporation.

My mother said he had every right to be.

Again he studied me as though debating whether I was worthy of a knighthood. Finally: "Are you trustworthy?"

My mother said I was the soul of honesty.

"That's right," I said.

The caller smiled for the first time. He told me I was a lucky young man. He admired my spunk. Too many young men thought life was all play. Those young men would not go far in this world. Only a young man willing to work and save and keep his face washed and his hair neatly combed could hope to come out on top in a world such as ours. Did I truly and sincerely believe that I was such a young man?

"He certainly does," said my mother.

"That's right," I said.

He said he had been so impressed by what he had seen of me that he was going to make me a representative of the Curtis Publishing Company. On the following Tuesday, he said, thirty freshly printed copies of the *Saturday Evening Post* would be delivered at our door. I would place these magazines, still damp with the ink of the presses, in a handsome canvas bag, sling it over my shoulder, and set forth through the streets to bring the best in journalism, fiction, and cartoons to the American public.

He had brought the canvas bag with him. He presented it with reverence fit for a chasuble. He showed me how to drape the sling over my left shoulder and across the chest so that the pouch lay easily accessible to my right hand, allowing the best in journalism, fiction, and cartoons to be swiftly extracted and sold to a citizenry whose happiness and security depended upon us soldiers of the free press.

The following Tuesday I raced home from school, put the canvas bag over my shoulder, dumped the magazines in, and, tilting to the left to balance their weight on my right hip, embarked on the highway of journalism.

We lived in Belleville, New Jersey, a commuter town at the northern fringe of Newark. It was 1932, the bleakest year of the Depression. My father had died two years before, leaving us with a few pieces of Sears, Roebuck furniture and not much else, and my mother had taken Doris and me to live with one of her younger brothers. This was my Uncle Allen. Uncle Allen had made something of himself by 1932.

As salesman for a soft-drink bottler in Newark, he had an income of $30 a week; wore pearl-gray spats, detachable collars, and a three-piece suit; was happily married; and took in threadbare relatives.

With my load of magazines I headed toward Belleville Avenue. That's where the people were. There were two filling stations at the intersection with Union Avenue, as well as an A&P, a fruit stand, a bakery, a barber shop, Zuccarelli's drugstore, and a diner shaped like a railroad car. For several hours I made myself highly visible, shifting position now and then from corner to corner, from shop window to shop window, to make sure everyone could see the heavy black lettering on the canvas bag that said THE SATURDAY EVENING POST. When the angle of the light indicated it was suppertime, I walked back to the house.

"How many did you sell, Buddy?" my mother asked.

35 "None." 35

"Where did you go?"

"The corner of Belleville and Union Avenues."

"What did you do?"

"Stood on the corner waiting for somebody to buy a *Saturday Evening Post*."

40 "You just stood there?" 40

"Didn't sell a single one."

"For God's sake, Russelll"

Uncle Allen intervened. "I've been thinking about it for some time," he said, "and I've about decided to take the *Post* regularly. Put me down as a regular customer." I handed him a magazine and he paid me a nickel. It was the first nickel I earned.

Afterwards my mother instructed me in salesmanship. I would have to ring doorbells, address adults with charming self-confidence, and break down resistance with a sales talk pointing out that no one, no matter how poor, could afford to be without the *Saturday Evening Post* in the home.

45 I told my mother I'd changed my mind about wanting to succeed 45 in the magazine business.

"If you think I'm going to raise a good-for-nothing," she replied, "you've got another think coming." She told me to hit the streets with the canvas bag and start ringing doorbells the instant school was out next day. When I objected that I didn't feel any aptitude for salesmanship, she asked how I'd like to lend her my leather belt so she could whack some sense into me, I bowed to superior will and entered journalism with a heavy heart.

My mother and I had fought this battle almost as long as I could remember. It probably started even before memory began, when I was a country child in northern Virginia and my mother, dissatisfied with my father's plain workman's life, determined that I would not grow up like him and his people, with calluses on their hands, overalls on their backs, and fourth-grade educations in their heads. She had fancier ideas of life's possibilities. Introducing me to the *Saturday Evening Post,* she was trying to wean me as early as possible from my father's world where men left with their lunch pails at sunup, worked with their hands until the grime ate into the pores, and died with a few sticks of mail-order furniture as their legacy. In my mother's vision of the better life there were desks and white collars, well-pressed suits, evenings of reading and lively talk, and perhaps—if a man were very, very lucky and hit the jackpot, really made something important of himself—perhaps there might be a fantastic salary of $5,000 a year to support a big house and a Buick with a rumble seat and a vacation in Atlantic City.

And so I set forth with my sack of magazines. I was afraid of the dogs that snarled behind the doors of potential buyers. I was timid about ringing the doorbells of strangers, relieved when no one came to the door, and scared when someone did. Despite my mother's instructions, I could not deliver an engaging sales pitch. When a door opened I simply asked, "Want to buy a *Saturday Evening Post?*" In Belleville few persons did. It was a town of 30,000 people, and most weeks I rang a fair majority of its doorbells. But I rarely sold my thirty copies. Some weeks I canvassed the entire town for six days and still had four or five unsold magazines on Monday evening; then I dreaded the coming of Tuesday morning, when a batch of thirty fresh *Saturday Evening Post*s was due at the front door.

"Better get out there and sell the rest of those magazines tonight," My mother would say.

I usually posted myself then at a busy intersection where a traffic light controlled commuter flow from Newark. When the light turned red I stood on the curb and shouted my sales pitch at the motorists.

"Want to buy a *Saturday Evening Post?*"

50

One rainy night when car windows were sealed against me I came back soaked and with not a single sale to report. My mother beckoned to Doris.

"Go back down there with Buddy and show him how to sell these magazines," she said.

Brimming with zest, Doris, who was then seven years old, returned with me to the corner. She took a magazine from the bag, and when the light turned red she strode to the nearest car and banged her small fist against the closed window. The driver, probably startled at what he took to be a midget assaulting his car, lowered the window to stare, and Doris thrust a *Saturday Evening Post* at him.

55 "You need this magazine," she piped, "and it only costs a nickel." 55

Her salesmanship was irresistible. Before the light changed half a dozen times she disposed of the entire batch. I didn't feel humiliated. To the contrary, I was so happy I decided to give her a treat. Leading her to the vegetable store on Belleville Avenue, I bought three apples, which cost a nickel, and gave her one.

"You shouldn't waste money," she said.

"Eat your apple." I bit into mine.

"You shouldn't eat before supper," she said. "It'll spoil your appetite."

60 Back at the house that evening, she dutifully reported me for 60 wasting a nickel. Instead of a scolding, I was rewarded with a pat on the back for having the good sense to buy fruit instead of candy. My mother reached into her bottomless supply of maxims and told Doris, "An apple a day keeps the doctor away."

By the time I was ten I had learned all my mother's maxims by heart. Asking to stay up past normal bedtime, I knew that a refusal would be explained with, "Early to bed and early to rise, makes a man healthy, wealthy, and wise." If I whimpered about having to get up early in the morning, I could depend on her to say, "The early bird gets the worm."

The one I most despised was, "If at first you don't succeed, try, try again." This was the battle cry with which she constantly sent me back into the hopeless struggle whenever I moaned that I had rung every doorbell in town and knew there wasn't a single potential buyer left in Belleville that week. After listening to my explanation, she handed me the canvas bag and said, "If at first you don't succeed . . ."

Three years in that job, which I would gladly have quit after the first day except for her insistence, produced at least one valuable result. My mother finally concluded that I would never make something of myself by pursuing a life in business and started considering careers that demanded less competitive zeal.

One evening when I was eleven I brought home a short "composition" on my summer vacation which the teacher had graded with an A. Reading it with her own schoolteacher's eye, my mother agreed that it was top-drawer seventh grade prose and complimented me. Nothing more was said about it immediately, but a new idea had taken life in her mind. Halfway through supper she suddenly interrupted the conversation.

65   "Buddy," she said, "maybe you could be a writer."   65

I clasped the idea to my heart. I had never met a writer, had shown no previous urge to write, and hadn't a notion how to become a writer, but I loved stories and thought that making up stories must surely be almost as much fun as reading them. Best of all, though, and what really gladdened my heart, was the ease of the writer's life. Writers did not have to trudge through the town peddling from canvas bags, defending themselves against angry dogs, being rejected by surly strangers. Writers did not have to ring doorbells. So far as I could make out, what writers did couldn't even be classified as work.

I was enchanted. Writers didn't have to have any gumption at all. I did not dare tell anybody for fear of being laughed at in the schoolyard, but secretly I decided that what I'd like to be when I grew up was a writer.

Mother Tongue
Amy Tan

Amy Tan was born in Oakland, California in 1952, several years after her mother and father immigrated from China. She was raised in various cities in the San Francisco Bay Area. When she was eight, her essay, "What the Library Means to Me," won first prize among elementary school participants, for which Tan received a transistor radio and publication in the local newspaper. Upon the deaths of her brother and father in 1967 and 1968 from brain tumors, the family began a haphazard journey through Europe, before settling in Montreux, Switzerland, where Tan graduated in her junior year in 1969.

For the next seven years, Tan attended five schools. She first went to Linfield College in McMinnville, Oregon, and there, on a blind date, met her future husband, Lou DeMattei. She followed him to San Jose, where she enrolled in San Jose City College. She next attended San Jose State University, and, while working two part-time jobs, she became an English honor's students and a President's Scholar, while carrying a semester course load of 21 units. In 1972 she graduated with honors, receiving a B.A. with a double major in English and Linguistics. She was awarded a scholarship to attend the Summer Linguistics Institute at the University of California, Santa Cruz. In 1973, she earned her M.A. in Linguistics, also from San Jose State University, and was then awarded a Graduate Minority Fellowship under the affirmative action program at the University of California, Berkeley, where she enrolled as a doctoral student in linguistics.

First published in *Threepenny Review*, 1990. Copyright © 1990 by Amy Tan.

1   I am not a scholar of English or literature. I cannot give you much   1
more than personal opinions on the English language and its variations in this country or others.

I am a writer. And by that definition, I am someone who has always loved language. I am fascinated by language in daily life. I spend
a great deal of my time thinking about the power of language—the
way it can evoke an emotion, a visual image, a complex idea, or a simple truth. Language is the tool of my trade. And I use them all—all
the Englishes I grew up with.

Recently, I was made keenly aware of the different Englishes I do
use. I was giving a talk to a large group of people, the same talk I had
already given to half a dozen other groups. The nature of the talk was
about my writing, my life, and my book, *The Joy Luck Club*. The talk
was going along well enough, until I remembered one major difference that made the whole talk sound wrong. My mother was in the
room. And it was perhaps the first time she had heard me give a
lengthy speech, using the kind of English I have never used with her.
I was saying things like, "The intersection of memory upon imagination" and "There is an aspect of my fiction that relates to thus-and-
thus"—a speech filled with carefully wrought grammatical phrases,
burdened, it suddenly seemed to me, with nominalized forms, past
perfect tenses, conditional phrases, all the forms of standard English
that I had learned in school and through books, the forms of English
I did not use at home with my mother.

Just last week, I was walking down the street with my mother, and
I again found myself conscious of the English I was using, and the
English I do use with her. We were talking about the price of new and
used furniture and I heard myself saying this: "Not waste money that
way." My husband was with us as well, and he didn't notice any switch
in my English. And then I realized why. It's because over the twenty
years we've been together I've often used that same kind of English
with him, and sometimes he even uses it with me. It has become our
language of intimacy, a different sort of English that relates to family
talk, the language I grew up with.

5   So you'll have some idea of what this family talk I heard sounds   5
like, I'll quote what my mother said during a recent conversation
which I videotaped and then transcribed. During this conversation,
my mother was talking about a political gangster in Shanghai who had
the same last name as her family's, Du, and how the gangster in his

early years wanted to be adopted by her family, which was rich by comparison. Later, the gangster became more powerful, far richer than my mother's family, and one day showed up at my mother's wedding to pay his respects. Here's what she said in part:

"Du Yusong having business like fruit stand. Like off the street kind. He is Du like Du Zong—but not Tsung-ming Island people. The local people call putong, the river east side, he belong to that side local people. That man want to ask Du Zong father take him in like become own family. Du Zong father wasn't look down on him, but didn't take seriously, until that man big like become a mafia. Now important person, very hard to inviting him. Chinese way, came only to show respect, don't stay for dinner. Respect for making big celebration, he shows up. Mean gives lots of respect. Chinese custom. Chinese social life that way. If too important won't have to stay too long. He come to my wedding. I didn't see, I heard it. I gone to boy's side, they have YMCA dinner. Chinese age I was nineteen."

You should know that my mother's expressive command of English belies how much she actually understands. She reads the *Forbes* report, listens to *Wall Street Week*, converses daily with her stockbroker, reads all of Shirley MacLaine's books with ease—all kinds of things I can't begin to understand. Yet some of my friends tell me they understand 50 percent of what my mother says. Some say they understand 80 to 90 percent. Some say they understand none of it, as if she were speaking pure Chinese. But to me, my mother's English is perfectly clear, perfectly natural. It's my mother tongue. Her language, as I hear it, is vivid, direct, full of observation and imagery. That was the language that helped shape the way I saw things, expressed things, made sense of the world.

Lately, I've been giving more thought to the kind of English my mother speaks. Like others, I have described it to people as "broken" or "fractured" English. But I wince when I say that. It has always bothered me that I can think of no way to describe it other than "broken," as if it were damaged and needed to be fixed, as if it lacked a certain wholeness and soundness. I've heard other terms used, "limited English," for example. But they seem just as bad, as if everything is limited, including people's perceptions of the limited English speaker.

I know this for a fact, because when I was growing up, my mother's "limited" English limited *my* perception of her. I was ashamed of her English. I believed that her English reflected the quality of what she had to say. That is, because she expressed them imperfectly her thoughts were imperfect. And I had plenty of empirical evidence to support me: the fact that people in department stores, at banks, and at restaurants did not take her seriously, did not give her good service, pretended not to understand her, or even acted as if they did not hear her.

10　　My mother has long realized the limitations of her English as well. 　10
When I was fifteen, she used to have me call people on the phone to pretend I was she. In this guise, I was forced to ask for information or even to complain and yell at people who had been rude to her. One time it was a call to her stockbroker in New York. She had cashed out her small portfolio and it just so happened we were going to go to New York the next week, our very first trip outside California. I had to get on the phone and say in an adolescent voice that was not very convincing, "This is Mrs. Tan."

And my mother was standing in the back whispering loudly, "Why he don't send me check, already two weeks late. So mad he lie to me, losing me money."

And then I said in perfect English, "Yes, I'm getting rather concerned. You had agreed to send the check two weeks ago, but it hasn't arrived."

Then she began to talk more loudly. "What he want, I come to New York tell him front of his boss, you cheating me?" And I was trying to calm her down, make her be quiet, while telling the stockbroker, "I can't tolerate any more excuses. If I don't receive the check immediately, I am going to have to speak to your manager when I'm in New York next week." And sure enough, the following week there we were in front of this astonished stockbroker, and I was sitting there red-faced and quiet, and my mother, the real Mrs. Tan, was shouting at his boss in her impeccable broken English.

We used a similar routine just five days ago, for a situation that was far less humorous. My mother had gone to the hospital for an appointment, to find out about a benign brain tumor a CAT scan had revealed a month ago. She said she had spoken very good English, her best English, no mistakes. Still, she said, the hospital did not apologize when they said they had lost the CAT scan and she had come for nothing. She said they did not seem to have any sympathy when she told them she was anxious to know the exact diagnosis, since her husband and son had both died of brain tumors. She said they would not give her any more information until the next time and she would have to make another appointment for that. So she said she would not leave until the doctor called her daughter. She wouldn't budge. And when the doctor finally called her daughter, me, who spoke in perfect English—lo and behold—we had assurances the CAT scan would be found, promises that a conference call on Monday would be held, and apologies for any suffering my mother had gone through for a most regrettable mistake.

15   I think my mother's English almost had an effect on limiting my 15
possibilities in life as well. Sociologists and linguists probably will tell you that a person's developing language skills are more influenced by peers. But I do think that the language spoken in the family, especially in immigrant families which are more insular, plays a large role in shaping the language of the child. And I believe that it affected my results on achievement tests, IQ tests, and the SAT. While my English skills were never judged as poor, compared to math, English could not be considered my strong suit. In grade school I did moderately well, getting perhaps B's, sometimes B-pluses, in English and scoring perhaps in the sixtieth or seventieth percentile on achievement tests. But those scores were not good enough to override the opinion that my true abilities lay in math and science, because in those areas I achieved A's and scored in the ninetieth percentile or higher.

This was understandable. Math is precise, there is only one correct answer. Whereas, for me at least, the answers on English tests were always a judgment call, a matter of opinion and personal experience. Those tests were constructed around items like fill-in-the-blank sentence completion, Such as, "Even though Tom was _____, Mary thought he was _____." And the correct answer always seemed to be the most bland combinations of thoughts, for example, "Even though Tom was shy, Mary thought he was charming," with the grammatical structure "even though" limiting the correct answer to some sort of semantic opposites, so you wouldn't get answers like, Even though Tom was foolish, Mary thought he was ridiculous." Well, according to my mother, there were very few limitations as to what Tom could have been and what Mary might have thought of him. So I never did well on tests like that.

The same was true with word analogies, pairs of words in which you were supposed to find some sort of logical, semantic relationship—

for example, "*Sunset* is to *nightfall* as _____ is to _____."
And here you would be presented with a list of four possible pairs, one
of which showed the same kind of relationship: *red* is to *stoplight, bus*
is to *arrival, chills* is to *fever, yawn* is to *boring*. Well, I could never think
that way. I knew what the tests were asking, but I could not block out
of my mind the images already created by the first pair, "*sunset* is to
nightfall"—and I would see a burst of colors against a darkening sky,
the moon rising, the lowering of a curtain of stars. And all the other
pairs of words—red, bus, stoplight, boring—just threw up a mass of
confusing images, making it impossible for me to sort out something
as logical as saying: "A sunset precedes nightfall" is the same as "a chill
precedes a fever." The only way I would have gotten that answer right
would have been to imagine an associative situation, for example, my
being disobedient and staying out past sunset, catching a chill at night,
which turns into feverish pneumonia as punishment, which indeed did
happen to me.

I have been thinking about all this lately, about my mother's English,
about achievement tests. Because lately I've been asked, as a writer,
why there are not more Asian Americans represented in American literature. Why are there few Asian Americans enrolled in creative writing programs? Why do so many Chinese students go into engineering?
Well, these are broad sociological questions I can't begin to answer.
But I have noticed in surveys—in fact, just last week—that Asian students, as a whole, always do significantly better on math achievement
tests than in English. And this makes me think that there are other
Asian American students whose English spoken in the home might
also be described as "broken" or "limited." And perhaps they also have
teachers who are steering them away from writing and into math and
science, which is what happened to me.

    Fortunately, I happen to be rebellious in nature and enjoy the
challenge of disproving assumptions made about me. I became an
English major my first year in college, after being enrolled as pre-med.
I started writing nonfiction as a freelancer the week after I was told by
my former boss that writing was my worst skill and I should hone my
talents toward account management.

20   But it wasn't until 1985 that I finally began to write fiction. And 20
at first I wrote using what I thought to be wittily crafted sentences,
sentences that would finally prove I had mastery over the English

language. Here's an example from the first draft of a story that later made its way into *The Joy Luck Club,* but without this line: "That was my mental quandary in its nascent state." A terrible line, which I can barely pronounce.

Fortunately, for reasons I won't get into today, I later decided I should envision a reader for the stories I would write. And the reader I decided upon was my mother, because these were stories about mothers. So with this reader in mind—and in fact she did read my early drafts—I began to write stories using all the Englishes I grew up with: the English I spoke to my mother, which for lack of a better term might be described as "simple"; the English she used with me, which for lack of a better term might be described as "broken"; my translation of her Chinese, which could certainly be described as "watered down"; and what I imagined to be her translation of her Chinese if she could speak in perfect English, her internal language, and for that I sought to preserve the essence, but neither an English nor a Chinese structure. I wanted to capture what language ability tests can never reveal: her intent, her passion, her imagery, the rhythms of her speech and the nature of her thoughts.

Apart from what any critic had to say about my writing, I knew I had succeeded where it counted when my mother finished reading my book and gave me her verdict: "So easy to read."

Hearing Voices

Linda Hogan

Chickasaw native Linda Hogan (1947–) was born to a military family in Denver Colo. and grew up in Oklahoma. She received an MA in 1978 from the University of Colorado at Boulder. Early in her career she supported herself with freelance writing and a variety of jobs, including nurse's aide, dental assistant, library clerk, and waitress. Hogan's writing spans all genres: Among her poetry collections are Seeing Through the Sun *(1985) and* The Book of Medicines *(1993). Her 1981 collection,* Daughters, I Love You, *was inspired by her adoption of two children of Oglaga Lakota heritage. Hogan has also written several novels, including* Mean Spirit *(1991) and* Power *(1999), and the essay collection* Dwellings *(1995), a spiritual exploration of relationships between humans and the natural world. Her work is decidedly feminist, and her focus on environmental and anti-nuclear issues has contributed significantly to the development of contemporary Native American poetry. Hogan's poetry, essays, and short stories have been anthologized widely. She has served as writer-in-residence for the states of Colorado and Oklahoma and has taught at Colorado College, the University of Minnesota, and the University of Colorado. Among her numerous awards are a Guggenheim fellowship, the Five Civilized Tribes Playwriting Award for* A Piece of the Moon *(1980), and the Word-craft Circle Writer of the Year Award for her most recent work,* The Woman Who Watches Over the World. A Native Memoir *(2002). In this selection, Hogan explores the nature of her writing, considering herself part of a*

---

larger community of voices including animals, plants, and the earth itself.

1   When Barbara McClintock was awarded a Nobel Prize for   1
her work on gene transposition in corn plants, the most
striking thing about her was that she made her discoveries
by listening to what the corn spoke to her, by respecting the life of the
corn and "letting it come."

McClintock says she learned "the stories" of the plants. She
"heard" them. She watched the daily green journeys of growth from
earth toward sky and sun. She knew her plants in the way a healer or
mystic would have known them, from the inside, the inner voices of
corn and woman speaking to one another.

As an Indian woman, I come from a long history of people who
have listened to the language of this continent, people who have known
that corn grows with the songs and prayers of the people, that it has a
story to tell, that the world is alive. Both in oral traditions and in
mythology—the true language of inner life—account after account
tells of the stones giving guidance, the trees singing, the corn telling of
inner earth, the dragonfly offering up a tongue. This is true in the
European traditions as well: Psyche received direction from the reeds
and the ants, Orpheus knew the languages of earth, animals, and birds.

This intuitive and common language is what I seek for my writing, work in touch with the mystery and force of life, work that
speaks a few of the many voices around us, and it is important to me
that McClintock listened to the voices of corn. It is important to the
continuance of life that she told the truth of her method and that it
reminded us of where our strength, our knowing, and our sustenance
come from.

5   It is also poetry, this science, and I note how often scientific theo-   5
ries lead to the world of poetry and vision, theories telling us how
atoms that were stars have been transformed into our living, breathing bodies. And in these theories, or maybe they should be called stories, we begin to understand how we are each many people, including
the stars we once were, and how we are in essence the earth and the universe, how what we do travels clear around the earth and returns. In a
single moment of our living, there is our ancestral and personal history, our future, even our deaths planted in us and already growing

30

toward their fulfillment. The corn plants are there, and like all the rest we are forever merging our borders with theirs in the world collective.

Our very lives might depend on this listening. In the Chernobyl nuclear accident, the wind told the story that was being suppressed by the people. It gave away the truth. It carried the story of danger to other countries. It was a poet, a prophet, a scientist.

Sometimes, like the wind, poetry has its own laws speaking for the life of the planet. It is a language that wants to bring back together what the other words have torn apart. It is the language of life speaking through us about the sacredness of life.

This life speaking life is what I find so compelling about the work of poets such as Ernesto Cardenal, who is also a priest and was the Nicaraguan Minister of Culture. He writes: "The armadilloes are very happy with this government. . . . Not only humans desired liberation/the whole ecology wanted it." Cardenal has also written "The Parrots," a poem about caged birds who were being sent to the United States as pets for the wealthy, how the cages were opened, the parrots allowed back into the mountains and jungles, freed like the people, "and sent back to the land we were pulled from."

How we have been pulled from the land! And how poetry has worked hard to set us free, uncage us, keep us from split tongues that mimic the voices of our captors. It returns us to our land. Poetry is a string of words that parades without a permit. It is a lockbox of words to put an ear to as we try to crack the safe of language, listening for the right combination, the treasure inside. It is life resonating. It is sometimes called Prayer, Soothsaying, Complaint, Invocation, Proclamation, Testimony, Witness. Writing is and does all these things. And like that parade, it is illegitimately insistent on going its own way, on being part of the miracle of life, telling the story about what happened when we were cosmic dust, what it means to be stars listening to our human atoms.

But don't misunderstand me. I am not just a dreamer. I am also the practical type. A friend's father, watching the United States stage another revolution in another Third World country, said, "Why doesn't the government just feed people and then let the political chips fall where they may?" He was right. It was easy, obvious, even financially more reasonable to do that, to let democracy be chosen because it feeds hunger. I want my writing to be that simple, that clear and direct. Likewise, I feel it is not enough for me just to write, but I need to live it, to be informed by it. I have found over the years that my work has more courage than I do. It has more wisdom. It teaches me, leads me places I never knew I was heading. And it is about a new way of living, of being in the world.

I was on a panel recently where the question was raised whether we thought literature could save lives. The audience, book people, smiled expectantly with the thought. I wanted to say, Yes, it saves lives. But I couldn't speak those words. It saves spirits maybe, hearts. It changes minds, but for me writing is an incredible privilege. When I sit down at the desk, there are other women who are hungry, homeless. I don't want to forget that, that the world of matter is still there to be reckoned with. This writing is a form of freedom most other people do not have. So, when I write, I feel a responsibility, a commitment to other humans and to the animal and plant communities as well.

Still, writing has changed me. And there is the powerful need we all have to tell a story, each of us with a piece of the whole pattern to complete. As Alice Walker says, We are all telling part of the same story, and as Sharon Olds has said, Every writer is a cell on the body politic of America.

Another Nobel Prize laureate is Betty William, a Northern Ireland co-winner of the 1977 Peace Prize. I heard her speak about how, after witnessing the death of children, she stepped outside in the middle of the night and began knocking on doors and yelling, behaviors that would have earned her a diagnosis of hysteria in our own medical circles. She knocked on doors that might have opened with weapons pointing in her face, and she cried out, "What kind of people have we become that we would allow children to be killed on our streets?" Within four hours the city was awake, and there were sixteen thousand names on petitions for peace. Now, that woman's work is a lesson to those of us who deal with language, and to those of us who are dealt into silence. She used language to begin the process of peace. This is the living, breathing power of the word. It is poetry. So are the names of those who signed the petitions. Maybe it is this kind of language that saves lives.

Writing begins for me with survival, with life and with freeing life, saving life, speaking life. It is work that speaks what can't be easily said. It originates from a compelling desire to live and be alive. For me, it is sometimes the need to speak for other forms of life, to take the side of human life, even our sometimes frivolous living, and our grief-filled living, our joyous living, our violent living, busy living our peaceful living. It is about possibility. It is based in the world of matter. I am interested in how something small turns into an image that is large and strong with resonance, where the ordinary becomes beautiful. I believe the divine, the magic, is here in the weeds at our feet, unacknowledged. What a world this is. Where else could water rise up to the sky, turn into snow crystals, magnificently brought together, fall from the sky all around us, pile up billions deep, and catch the small sparks of sunlight as they return again to water?

15   These acts of magic happen all the time; in Chaco Canyon, my   15
sister has seen a kiva, a ceremonial room in the earth, that is in the center of the canyon. This place has been uninhabited for what seems like forever. It has been without water. In fact, there are theories that the ancient people disappeared when they journeyed after water. In the center of it a corn plant was growing. It was all alone and it had been there since the ancient ones, the old ones who came before us all, those people who wove dog hair into belts, who witnessed the painting of flute players on the seeping canyon walls, who knew the stories of corn. And there was one corn plant growing out of the holy place. It planted itself yearly. With no water, no person to care for it, no overturning of the soil, this corn plant rises up to tell its story, and that's what this poetry is.

The Struggle to Be an All-American Girl

Elizabeth Wong

Elizabeth Wong, a playwright and television writer, grew up in Chinatown in Los Angeles. Although she resisted, her mother insisted that she learn the Chinese language and culture when she was in grade school. Educated at the University of Southern California (1980) and New York University (1991), Wong has worked as a reporter and taught in the theater department at Bowdoin College. In this essay, which was first published in the Los Angeles Times, *Wong recounts her childhood rebellion against learning Chinese and her adult regret of her assimilation into American culture.*

1   It's still there, the Chinese school on Yale Street where my brother and I used to go. Despite the new coat of paint and the high wire fence, the school I knew 10 years ago remains remarkably, stoically the same.

Every day at 5 P.M., instead of playing with our fourth- and fifth-grade friends or sneaking out to the empty lot to hunt ghosts and animal bones, my brother and I had to go to Chinese school. No amount of kicking, screaming, or pleading could dissuade my mother, who was solidly determined to have us learn the language of our heritage.

Forcibly, she walked us the seven long, hilly blocks from our home to school, depositing our defiant tearful faces before the stern principal. My only memory of him is that he swayed on his heels like a palm tree, and he always clasped his impatient twitching hands behind his back. I recognized him as a repressed maniacal child killer, and knew that if we ever saw his hands we'd be in big trouble.

Originally appeared in the *Los Angeles Times*.

We all sat in little chairs in an empty auditorium. The room smelled like Chinese medicine, an imported faraway mustiness. Like ancient mothballs or dirty closets. I hated that smell. I favored crisp new scents. Like the soft French perfume that my American teacher wore in public school.

5   There was a stage far to the right, flanked by an American flag and the flag of the Nationalist Republic of China, which was also red, white and blue but not as pretty.

Although the emphasis at the school was mainly language—speaking, reading, writing—the lessons always began with an exercise in politeness. With the entrance of the teacher, the best student would tap a bell and everyone would get up, kowtow, and chant, "Sing san ho," the phonetic for "How are you, teacher?"

Being ten years old, I had better things to learn than ideographs copied painstakingly in lines that ran right to left from the tip of a *moc but,* a real ink pen that had to be held in an awkward way if blotches were to be avoided. After all, I could do the multiplication tables, name the satellites of Mars, and write reports on *Little Women* and *Black Beauty.* Nancy Drew, my favorite book heroine, never spoke Chinese.

The language was a source of embarrassment. More times than not, I had tried to disassociate myself from the nagging loud voice that followed me wherever I wandered in the nearby American supermarket outside Chinatown. The voice belonged to my grandmother, a fragile woman in her seventies who could outshout the best of the street vendors. Her humor was raunchy, her Chinese rhythmless, patternless. It was quick, it was loud, it was unbeautiful. It was not like the quiet, lilting romance of French or the gentle refinement of the American South. Chinese sounded pedestrian. Public.

In Chinatown, the comings and goings of hundreds of Chinese on their daily tasks sounded chaotic and frenzied. I did not want to be thought of as mad, as talking gibberish. When I spoke English, people nodded at me, smiled sweetly, said encouraging words. Even the people in my culture would cluck and say that I'd do well in life. "My, doesn't she move her lips fast," they would say, meaning that I'd be able to keep up with the world outside Chinatown.

10   My brother was even more fanatical than I about speaking English. He was especially hard on my mother, criticizing her, often cruelly, for her pidgin speech—smatterings of Chinese scattered like chop

suey in her conversation. "It's not 'What it is,' Mom," he'd say in exasperation. "It's 'What *is* it, what *is* it, what *is* it!' " Sometimes Mom might leave out an occasional "the" or "a," or perhaps a verb of being. He would stop her in mid-sentence: "Say it again, Mom. Say it right." When he tripped over his own tongue, he'd blame it on her: "See, Mom, it's all your fault. You set a bad example."

What infuriated my mother most was when my brother cornered her on her consonants, especially "r." My father had played a cruel joke on Mom by assigning her an American name that her tongue wouldn't allow her to say. No matter how hard she tried, "Ruth" always ended up "Luth" or "Roof."

After two years of writing with a *moc but* and reciting words with multiples of meanings, I finally was granted a cultural divorce. I was permitted to stop Chinese school.

I thought of myself as multicultural. I preferred tacos to egg rolls; I enjoyed Cinco de Mayo[1] more than Chinese New Year.

At last, I was one of you; I wasn't one of them.

Sadly, I still am.

15   15

---

[1]Fifth of May, Mexican national holiday marking Mexico's victory over France at Puebla in 1862.

From Silence to Words: Writing as Struggle

Min-zhan Lu

Min-zhan Lu (1946–) was born in China. Lu, who grew up speaking English as well as a number of Chinese dialects, has taught composition and literary criticism at Drake University. She has published both academic articles related to composition issues and articles about her life in China. This article, published in College English *in 1987, relates Lu's challenges acquiring literacy in both China and the United States and how those challenges have affected her writing and teaching.*

Imagine that you enter a parlor. You come late. When you arrive, others have long preceded you, and they are engaged in a heated discussion. . . .You listen for a while, until you decide that you have caught the tenor of the argument; then you put in your oar. Someone answers; you answer him; another comes to your defense; another aligns himself against you, to either the embarrassment or gratification of your opponent, depending upon the quality of your ally's assistance. However, the discussion is interminable. The hour grows late, you must depart. And you do depart, with the discussion still vigorously in progress.

     —Kenneth Burke, The Philosophy of Literary Form

Men are not built in silence, but in word, in work, in action-reflection.

     —Paulo Freire, Pedagogy of the Oppressed

From *College English,* April, 1987. Copyright © 1987 by the National Council of Teachers of English.

1   **M**y mother withdrew into silence two months before she 1 died. A few nights before she fell silent, she told me she regretted the way she had raised me and my sisters. I knew she was referring to the way we had been brought up in the midst of two conflicting worlds—the world of home, dominated by the ideology of the Western humanistic tradition, and the world of a society dominated by Mao Tse-tung's Marxism. My mother had devoted her life to our education, an education she knew had made us suffer political persecution during the Cultural Revolution. I wanted to find a way to convince her that, in spite of the persecution, I had benefited from the education she had worked so hard to give me. But I was silent. My understanding of my education was so dominated by memories of confusion and frustration that I was unable to reflect on what I could have gained from it.

This paper is my attempt to fill up that silence with words, words I didn't have then, words that I have since come to by reflecting on my earlier experience as a student in China and on my recent experience as a composition teacher in the United States. For in spite of the frustration and confusion I experienced growing up caught between two conflicting worlds, the conflict ultimately helped me to grow as a reader and writer. Constantly having to switch back and forth between the discourse of home and that of school made me sensitive and self-conscious about the struggle I experienced every time I tried to read, write, or think in either discourse. Eventually, it led me to search for constructive uses for such struggle.

From early childhood, I had identified the differences between home and the outside world by the different languages I used in each. My parents had wanted my sisters and me to get the best education they could conceive of—Cambridge. They had hired a live-in tutor, a Scot, to make us bilingual. I learned to speak English with my parents, my tutor, and my sisters. I was allowed to speak Shanghai dialect only with the servants. When I was four (the year after the Communist Revolution of 1949), my parents sent me to a local private school where I learned to speak, read, and write in a new language—Standard Chinese, the official written language of New China.

In those days I moved from home to school, from English to Standard Chinese to Shanghai dialect, with no apparent friction. I spoke each language with those who spoke the language. All seemed quite "natural"—servants spoke only Shanghai dialect because they were

38

servants; teachers spoke Standard Chinese because they were teachers; languages had different words because they were different languages. I thought of English as my family language, comparable to the many strange dialects I didn't speak but had often heard some of my classmates speak with their families. While I was happy to have a special family language, until second grade I didn't feel that my family language was any different than some of my classmates' family dialects.

My second grade homeroom teacher was a young graduate from a missionary school. When she found out I spoke English, she began to practice her English on me. One day she used English when asking me to run an errand for her. As I turned to close the door behind me, I noticed the puzzled faces of my classmates. I had the same sensation I had often experienced when some stranger in a crowd would turn on hearing me speak English. I was more intensely pleased on this occasion, however, because suddenly I felt that my family language had been singled out from the family languages of my classmates. Since we were not allowed to speak any dialect other than Standard Chinese in the classroom, having my teacher speak English to me in class made English an official language of the classroom. I began to take pride in my ability to speak it.

This incident confirmed in my mind what my parents had always told me about the importance of English to one's life. Time and again they had told me of how my paternal grandfather, who was well versed in classic Chinese, kept losing good-paying jobs because he couldn't speak English. My grandmother reminisced constantly about how she had slaved and saved to send my father to a first-rate missionary school. And we were made to understand that it was my father's fluent English that had opened the door to his success. Even though my family had always stressed the importance of English for my future, I used to complain bitterly about the extra English lessons we had to take after school. It was only after my homeroom teacher had "sanctified" English that I began to connect English with my education. I became a much more eager student in my tutorials.

What I learned from my tutorials seemed to enhance and reinforce what I was learning in my classroom. In those days each word had one meaning. One day I would be making a sentence at school: "The national flag of China is red." The next day I would recite at home, "My love is like a red, red rose." There seemed to be an agreement between the Chinese "red" and the English "red," and both corresponded to the patch of color printed next to the word. "Love" was my love for my mother at home and my love for my "motherland" at school; both "loves" meant how I felt about my mother. Having two loads of homework forced me to develop a quick memory for words and a sensitivity to form and style. What I learned in one language carried over to the other. I made sentences such as, "I saw a red, red rose among the green leaves," with both the English lyric and the classic Chinese lyric—red flower among green leaves—running through my mind, and I was praised by both teacher and tutor for being a good student.

Although my elementary schooling took place during the fifties, I was almost oblivious to the great political and social changes happening around me. Years later, I read in my history and political philosophy textbooks that the fifties were a time when "China was making a transition from a semi-feudal, semi-capitalist, and semi-colonial country into a socialist country," a period in which "the Proletarians were breaking into the educational territory dominated by Bourgeois Intellectuals." While people all over the country were being officially classified into Proletarians, Petty-bourgeois, National-bourgeois, Poor-peasants, and Intellectuals, and were trying to adjust to their new social identities, my parents were allowed to continue the upper middle-class life they had established before the 1949 Revolution because of my father's affiliation with British firms. I had always felt that my family was different from the families of my classmates, but I didn't perceive society's view of my family until the summer vacation before I entered high school.

First, my aunt was caught by her colleagues talking to her husband over the phone in English. Because of it, she was criticized and almost labeled a Rightist. (This was the year of the Anti-Rightist movement, a movement in which the Intellectuals became the target of the "socialist class-struggle.") I had heard others telling my mother that she was foolish to teach us English when Russian had replaced English as the "official" foreign language. I had also learned at school that the American and British Imperialists were the arch-enemies of New China. Yet I had made no connection between the arch-enemies and the English our family spoke. What happened to my aunt forced the connection on me. I began to see my parents' choice of a family language as an anti-Revolutionary act and was alarmed that I had participated in such an act. From then on, I took care not to use English outside home and to conceal my knowledge of English from my new classmates.

10 Certain words began to play important roles in my new life at the junior high. On the first day of school, we were handed forms to fill out with our parents' class, job, and income. Being one of the few people not employed by the government, my father had never been officially classified. Since he was a medical doctor, he told me to put him down as an Intellectual. My homeroom teacher called me into the office a couple of days afterwards and told me that my father couldn't be an Intellectual if his income far exceeded that of a Capitalist. He also told me that since my father worked for Foreign Imperialists, my father should be classified as an Imperialist Lackey. The teacher looked nonplussed when I told him that my father couldn't be an Imperialist Lackey because he was a medical doctor. But I could tell from the way he took notes on my form that my father's job had put me in an unfavorable position in his eyes.

The Standard Chinese term "class" was not a new word for me. Since first grade, I had been taught sentences such as, "The Working class are the masters of New China." I had always known that it was good to be a worker, but until then, I had never felt threatened for not being one. That fall, "class" began to take on a new meaning for me. I noticed a group of Working-class students and teachers at school. I was made to understand that because of my class background, I was excluded from that group.

Another word that became important was "consciousness." One of the slogans posted in the school building read, "Turn our students into future Proletarians with socialist consciousness and education!" For several weeks we studied this slogan in our political philosophy course, a subject I had never had in elementary school. I still remember the definition of "socialist consciousness" that we were repeatedly tested on through the years: "Socialist consciousness is a person's political soul. It is the consciousness of the Proletarians represented by Marxist Mao Tse-tung thought. It takes expression in one's action, language, and lifestyle. It is the task of every Chinese student to grow up into a Proletarian with a socialist consciousness so that he can serve the people and the motherland." To make the abstract concept accessible to us, our teacher pointed out that the immediate task for students from Working-class families was to strengthen their socialist consciousnesses. For those of us who were from other class backgrounds, the task was to turn ourselves into Workers with socialist consciousnesses. The teacher never explained exactly how we were supposed to "turn" into Workers. Instead, we were given samples of the ritualistic annual plans we had to write at the beginning of each term. In these plans, we performed "self-criticism" on our consciousnesses and made vows to turn ourselves into Workers with socialist consciousnesses. The teacher's division between those who did and those who didn't have a socialist consciousness led me to reify the notion of "consciousness" into a thing one possesses. I equated this intangible "thing" with a concrete way of dressing, speaking, and writing. For instance, I never doubted that my political philosophy teacher had a socialist consciousness because she was from a steelworker's family (she announced this the first day of class) and was a party member who wore grey cadre suits and talked like a philosophy textbook. I noticed other things about her. She had beautiful eyes and spoke Standard Chinese with such a pure accent that I thought she should be a film star. But I was embarrassed that I had noticed things that ought not to have been associated with her. I blamed my observation on my Bourgeois consciousness.

At the same time, the way reading and writing were taught through memorization and imitation also encouraged me to reduce concepts and ideas to simple definitions. In literature and political philosophy classes, we were taught a large number of quotations from Marx, Lenin, and Mao Tse-tung. Each concept that appeared in these quotations came with a definition. We were required to memorize the definitions of the words along with the quotations. Every time I memorized a definition, I felt I had learned a word: "The national red flag symbolizes the blood shed by Revolutionary ancestors for our socialist cause"; "New China rises like a red sun over the eastern horizon." As I memorized these sentences, I reduced their metaphors to dictionary meanings: "red" meant "Revolution" and "red sun" meant "New China" in the "language" of the Working class. I learned mechanically but eagerly. I soon became quite fluent in this new language.

As school began to define me as a political subject, my parents tried to build up my resistance to the "communist poisoning" by exposing me to the "great books"—novels by Charles Dickens, Nathaniel Hawthorne, Emily Brontë, Jane Austen, and writers from around the turn of the century. My parents implied that these writers represented how I, their child, should read and write. My parents replaced the word "Bourgeois" with the word "cultured." They reminded me that I was in school only to learn math and science. I needed to pass the other courses to stay in school, but I was not to let the "Red doctrines" corrupt my mind. Gone were the days when I could innocently write, "I saw the red, red rose among the green leaves," collapsing, as I did, English and Chinese cultural traditions. "Red" came to mean Revolution at school, "the Commies" at home, and adultery in *The Scarlet Letter*. Since I took these symbols and metaphors as meanings natural to people of the same class, I abandoned my earlier definitions of English and Standard Chinese as the language of home and the language of school. I now defined English as the language of the Bourgeois and Standard Chinese as the language of the Working class. I thought of the language of the Working class as someone else's language and the language of the Bourgeois as my language. But I also believed that, although the language of the Bourgeois was my real language, I could and would adopt the language of the Working class when I was at school. I began to put on and take off my Working class language in the same way I put on and took off my school clothes to avoid being criticized for wearing Bourgeois clothes.

15   In my literature classes, I learned the Working-class formula for   15
reading. Each work in the textbook had a short "Author's Biography": "X X X, born in 19—in the province of X X X, is from a Worker's family. He joined the Revolution in 19—. He is a Revolutionary realist with a passionate love for the Party and Chinese Revolution. His work expresses the thoughts and emotions of the masses and sings praise to the prosperous socialist construction on all fronts of China." The teacher used the "Author's Biography" as a yardstick to measure the texts. We were taught to locate details in the texts that illustrated these summaries, such as words that expressed Workers' thoughts and emotions or events that illustrated the Workers' lives.

I learned a formula for Working-class writing in the composition classes. We were given sample essays and told to imitate them. The theme was always about how the collective taught the individual a lesson. I would write papers about labor-learning experiences or school-cleaning days, depending on the occasion of the collective activity closest to the assignment. To make each paper look different, I dressed it up with details about the date, the weather, the environment, or the appearance of the Master-worker who had taught me "the lesson." But as I became more and more fluent in the generic voice of the Working-class Student, I also became more and more self-conscious about the language we used at home.

For instance, in senior high we began to have English classes ("to study English for the Revolution," as the slogan on the cover of the textbook said), and I was given my first Chinese-English dictionary. There I discovered the English version of the term "class-struggle." (The Chinese characters for a school "class" and for a social "class" are different.) I had often used the English word "class" at home in sentences such as, "So and so has class," but I had not connected this sense of "class" with "class-struggle." Once the connection was made, I heard a second layer of meaning every time someone at home said a person had "class." The expression began to mean the person had the style and sophistication characteristic of the bourgeoisie. The word lost its innocence. I was uneasy about hearing that second layer of meaning because I was sure my parents did not hear the word that way. I felt that therefore I should not be hearing it that way either. Hearing the second layer of meaning made me wonder if I was losing my English.

My suspicion deepened when I noticed myself unconsciously merging and switching between the "reading" of home and the "reading" of school. Once I had to write a report on *The Revolutionary Family,* a book about an illiterate woman's awakening and growth as a Revolutionary through the deaths of her husband and all her children for the cause of the Revolution. In one scene the woman deliberated over whether or not she should encourage her youngest son to join the Revolution. Her memory of her husband's death made her afraid to encourage her son. Yet she also remembered her earlier married life and the first time her husband tried to explain the meaning of the Revolution to her. These memories made her feel she should encourage her son to continue the cause his father had begun.

I was moved by this scene. "Moved" was a word my mother and sisters used a lot when we discussed books. Our favorite moments in novels were moments of what I would now call internal conflict, moments which we said "moved" us. I remember that we were "moved" by Jane Eyre when she was torn between her sense of ethics, which compelled her to leave the man she loved, and her impulse to stay with the only man who had ever loved her. We were also moved by Agnes in *David Copperfield* because of the way she restrained her love for

David so that he could live happily with the woman he loved. My standard method of doing a book report was to model it on the review by the Publishing Bureau and to dress it up with detailed quotations from the book. The review of *The Revolutionary Family* emphasized the woman's Revolutionary spirit. I decided to use the scene that had moved me to illustrate this point. I wrote the report the night before it was due. When I had finished, I realized I couldn't possibly hand it in. Instead of illustrating her Revolutionary spirit, I had dwelled on her internal conflict, which could be seen as a moment of weak sentimentality that I should never have emphasized in a Revolutionary heroine. I wrote another report, taking care to illustrate the grandeur of her Revolutionary spirit by expanding on a quotation in which she decided that if the life of her son could change the lives of millions of sons, she should not begrudge his life for the cause of Revolution. I handed in my second version but kept the first in my desk.

20   I never showed it to anyone. I could never show it to people outside my family, because it had deviated so much from the reading enacted by the jacket review. Neither could I show it to my mother or sisters, because I was ashamed to have been so moved by such a "Revolutionary" book. My parents would have been shocked to learn that I could like such a book in the same way they liked Dickens. Writing this book report increased my fear that I was losing the command over both the "language of home" and the "language of school" that I had worked so hard to gain. I tried to remind myself that, if I could still tell when my reading or writing sounded incorrect, then I had retained my command over both languages. Yet I could no longer be confident of my command over either language because I had discovered that when I was not careful—or even when I was—my reading and writing often surprised me with its impurity. To prevent such impurity, I became very suspicious of my thoughts when I read or wrote. I was always asking myself why I was using this word, how I was using it, always afraid that I wasn't reading or writing correctly. What confused and frustrated me most was that I could not figure out why I was no longer able to read or write correctly without such painful deliberation.   20

I continued to read only because reading allowed me to keep my thoughts and confusion private. I hoped that somehow, if I watched myself carefully, I would figure out from the way I read whether I had really mastered the "languages." But writing became a dreadful chore. When I tried to keep a diary, I was so afraid that the voice of school might slip in that I could only list my daily activities. When I wrote for school, I worried that my Bourgeois sensibilities would betray me.

The more suspicious I became about the way I read and wrote, the more guilty I felt for losing the spontaneity with which I had learned to "use" these "languages." Writing the book report made me feel that my reading and writing in the "language" of either home or school could not be free of the interference of the other. But I was unable to acknowledge, grasp, or grapple with what I was experiencing, for both my parents and my teachers had suggested that, if I were a good student, such interference would and should not take place. I assumed that once I had "acquired" a discourse, I could simply switch it on and off every time I read and wrote as I would some electronic tool. Furthermore, I expected my readings and writings to come out in their correct forms whenever I switched the proper discourse on. I still regarded the discourse of home as natural and the discourse of school alien, but I never had doubted before that I could acquire both and switch them on and off according to the occasion.

When my experience in writing conflicted with what I thought should happen when I used each discourse, I rejected my experience because it contradicted what my parents and teachers had taught me. I shied away from writing to avoid what I assumed I should not experience. But trying to avoid what should not happen did not keep it from recurring whenever I had to write. Eventually my confusion and frustration over these recurring experiences compelled me to search for an explanation: how and why had I failed to learn what my parents and teachers had worked so hard to teach me?

I now think of the internal scene for my reading and writing about *The Revolutionary Family* as a heated discussion between myself, the voices of home, and those of school. The review on the back of the book, the sample student papers I came across in my composition classes, my philosophy teacher—these I heard as voices of one group. My parents and my home readings were the voices of an opposing group. But the conversation between these opposing voices in the internal scene of my writing was not as polite and respectful as the parlor scene Kenneth Burke has portrayed (see epigraph). Rather, these voices struggled to dominate the discussion, constantly incorporating, dismissing, or suppressing the arguments of each other, like the battles between the hegemonic and counter-hegemonic forces described in Raymond Williams' *Marxism and Literature* (108–14).

25   When I read *The Revolutionary Family* and wrote the first version   25
of my report, I began with a quotation from the review. The voices of
both home and school answered, clamoring to be heard. I tried to listen to one group and turn a deaf ear to the other. Both persisted. I negotiated my way through these conflicting voices, now agreeing with
one, now agreeing with the other. I formed a reading out of my interaction with both. Yet I was afraid to have done so because both
home and school had implied that I should speak in unison with only
one of these groups and stand away from the discussion rather than
participate in it.

My teachers and parents had persistently called my attention to
the intensity of the discussion taking place on the external social scene.
The story of my grandfather's failure and my father's success had from
my early childhood made me aware of the conflict between Western
and traditional Chinese cultures. My political education at school
added another dimension to the conflict; the war of Marxist-Maoism
against them both. Yet when my parents and teachers called my attention to the conflict, they stressed the anxiety of having to live
through China's transformation from a semi-feudal, semi-capitalist,
and semi-colonial society to a socialist one. Acquiring the discourse of
the dominant group was, to them, a means of seeking alliance with
that group and thus of surviving the whirlpool of cultural currents
around them. As a result, they modeled their pedagogical practices on
this utilitarian view of language. Being the eager student, I adopted
this view of language as a tool for survival. It came to dominate my
understanding of the discussion on the social and historical scene and
to restrict my ability to participate in that discussion.

To begin with, the metaphor of language as a tool for survival led
me to be passive in my use of discourse, to be a bystander in the discussion. In Burke's "parlor," everyone is involved in the discussion. As
it goes on through history, what we call "communal discourses"—arguments specific to particular political, social, economic, ethnic, sexual, and family groups—form, re-form and transform. To use a
discourse in such a scene is to participate in the argument and to contribute to the formation of the discourse. But when I was growing up,
I could not take on the burden of such an active role in the discussion. For both home and school presented the existent conventions of
the discourse each taught me as absolute laws for my action. They
turned verbal action into a tool, a set of conventions produced and

shaped prior to and outside of my own verbal acts. Because I saw language as a tool, I separated the process of producing the tool from the process of using it. The tool was made by someone else and was then acquired and used by me. How the others made it before I acquired it determined and guaranteed what it produced when I used it. I imagined that the more experienced and powerful members of the community were the ones responsible for making the tool. They were the ones who participated in the discussion and fought with opponents. When I used what they made, their labor and accomplishments would ensure the quality of my reading and writing. By using it, I could survive the heated discussion. When my immediate experience in writing the book report suggested that knowing the conventions of school did not guarantee the form and content of my report, when it suggested that I had to write the report with the work and responsibility I had assigned to those who wrote book reviews in the Publishing bureau, I thought I had lost the tool I had earlier acquired.

Another reason I could not take up an active role in the argument was that my parents and teachers contrived to provide a scene free of conflict for practicing my various languages. It was as if their experience had made them aware of the conflict between their discourse and other discourses and of the struggle involved in reproducing the conventions of any discourse on a scene where more than one discourse exists. They seemed convinced that such conflict and struggle would overwhelm someone still learning the discourse. Home and school each contrived a purified space where only one discourse was spoken and heard. In their choice of textbooks, in the way they spoke, and in the way they required me to speak, each jealously silenced any voice that threatened to break the unison of the scene. The homogeneity of home and of school implied that only one discourse could and should be relevant in each place. It led me to believe I should leave behind, turn a deaf ear to, or forget the discourse of the other when I crossed the boundary dividing them. I expected myself to set down one discourse whenever I took up another just as I would take off or put on a particular set of clothes for school or home.

Despite my parents' and teachers' attempts to keep home and school discrete, the internal conflict between the two discourses continued whenever I read or wrote. Although I tried to suppress the voice of one discourse in the name of the other, having to speak aloud in the voice I had just silenced each time I crossed the boundary kept both voices active in my mind. Every "I think . . . " from the voice of home or school brought forth a "However . . . " or a "But. . ." from the voice of the opponents. To identify with the voice of home or school, I had to negotiate through the conflicting voices of both by re-stating, taking back, qualifying my thoughts. I was unconsciously doing so when I did my book report. But I could not use the interaction comfortably and constructively. Both my parents and my teachers had implied that my job was to prevent that interaction from happening. My sense of having failed to accomplish what they had taught silenced me.

30   To use the interaction between the discourses of home and school   30 constructively, I would have to have seen reading or writing as a process in which I worked my way towards a stance through a dialectical process of identification and division. To identify with an ally, I would have to have grasped the distance between where he or she stood and where I was positioning myself. In taking a stance against an opponent, I would have to have grasped where my stance identified with the stance of my allies. Teetering along the "wavering line of pressure and counter-pressure" from both allies and opponents, I might have worked my way towards a stance of my own (Burke, *A Rhetoric of Motives*, 23). Moreover, I would have to have understood that the voices in my mind, like the participants in the parlor scene, were in constant flux. As I came into contact with new and different groups of people or read different books, voices entered and left. Each time I read or wrote, the stance I negotiated out of these voices would always be at some distance from the stances I worked out in my previous and my later readings or writings.

I could not conceive such a form of action for myself because I saw reading and writing as an expression of an established stance. In delineating the conventions of a discourse, my parents and teachers had synthesized the stance they saw as typical for a representative member of the community. Burke calls this the stance of a "god" or the "prototype"; Williams calls it the "official" or "possible" stance of the community. Through the metaphor of the survival tool, my parents and teachers had led me to assume I could automatically reproduce the official stance of the discourse I used. Therefore, when I did my book report on *The Revolutionary Family*, I expected my knowledge of the official stance set by the book review to ensure the actual stance of my report. As it happened, I began by trying to take the official stance of the review. Other voices interrupted. I answered back. In the process, I worked out a stance approximate but not identical to the official stance I began with. Yet the experience of having to labor to realize my knowledge of the official stance or to prevent myself from wandering away from it frustrated and confused me. For even though I had been actually reading and writing in a Burkean scene, I was afraid to participate actively in the discussion. I assumed it was my role to survive by staying out of it.

Not long ago, my daughter told me that it bothered her to hear her friend "talk wrong." Having come to the United States from China with little English, my daughter has become sensitive to the way English, as spoken by her teachers, operates. As a result, she has amazed her teachers with her success in picking up the language and in adapting to life at school. Her concern to speak the English taught in the classroom "correctly" makes her uncomfortable when she hears people using "ain't" or double negatives, which her teacher considers "improper." I see in her the me that had eagerly learned and used the discourse of the Working class at school. Yet while I was torn between the two conflicting worlds of school and home, she moves with seeming ease from the conversations she hears over the dinner table to her teacher's words in the classroom. My husband and I are proud of the good work she does at school. We are glad she is spared the kinds of conflict between home and school I experienced at her age. Yet as we watch her becoming more and more fluent in the language of the classroom, we wonder if, by enabling her to "survive" school, her very fluency will silence her when the scene of her reading and writing expands beyond that of the composition classroom.

For when I listen to my daughter, to students, and to some composition teachers talking about the teaching and learning of writing, I am often alarmed by the degree to which the metaphor of a survival tool dominates their understanding of language as it once dominated my own. I am especially concerned with the way some composition classes focus on turning the classroom into a monological scene for the students' reading and writing. Most of our students live in a world similar to my daughter's, somewhere between the purified world of the classroom and the complex world of my adolescence. When composition classes encourage these students to ignore those voices that seem irrelevant to the purified world of the classroom, most students are often able to do so without much struggle. Some of them are so adept at doing it that the whole process has for them become automatic.

However, beyond the classroom and beyond the limited range of these students' immediate lives lies a much more complex and dynamic social and historical scene. To help these students become actors in such a scene, perhaps we need to call their attention to voices that may seem irrelevant to the discourse we teach rather than encourage them to shut them out. For example, we might intentionally complicate the classroom scene by bringing into it discourses that stand at varying distances from the one we teach. We might encourage students to explore ways of practicing the conventions of the discourse they are learning by negotiating through these conflicting voices. We could also encourage them to see themselves as responsible for forming or transforming as well as preserving the discourse they are learning.

35 As I think about what we might do to complicate the external and internal scenes of our students' writing, I hear my parents and teachers saying: "Not now. Keep them from the wrangle of the marketplace until they have acquired the discourse and are skilled at using it." And I answer: "Don't teach them to 'survive' the whirlpool of crosscurrents by avoiding it. Use the classroom to moderate the currents. Moderate the currents, but teach them from the beginning to struggle." When I think of the ways in which the teaching of reading and writing as classroom activities can frustrate the development of students, I am almost grateful for the overwhelming complexity of the circumstances in which I grew up. For it was this complexity that kept me from losing sight of the effort and choice involved in reading or writing with and through a discourse.

References

Burke, Kenneth. *The Philosophy of Literary Form: Studies in Symbolic Action.* 2nd ed. Baton Rouge: Louisiana State UP, 1967.

———. *A Rhetoric of Motives.* Berkeley: U of California P, 1969.

Freire, Paulo. *Pedagogy of the Oppressed.* Trans. M. B. Ramos. New York: Continuum, 1970.

Williams, Raymond. *Marxism and Literature.* New York: Oxford UP, 1977.

Lived Literacy Resources from T.E.D.com

On Creativity by Amy Tan
Gaming Can Make the World a Better Place by Jone
McGonigal

Cultural Literacies

Cultural Literacies: Introduction

The readings in this section present some cultural practices that we think of people being more or less literate about: sports, school, music, ethnic-based gender stereotypes, and social concepts (meritocracy). As you read continue to think about the invention strategies these writers use to create their texts. For example, some writers in this section connect particular practices—like the leisurely pace of baseball—to larger cultural realities—such as the slower pace of life and prevalence of agricultural economies during the time that baseball becomes a national pastime.

These readings also give you an opportunity to think seriously about what new kinds of organizational plans you are introduced to while reading. In "Football Red and Base Ball Green," for example, Murray Ross chooses to discuss one sport at length before moving to the next sport. This allows him to make the issues such as concepts of time and the character of athletes, and what they imply about the larger topic of culture, easier to integrate throughout his essay. As you read, think about what other organizing strategies are at work in the essays. Furthermore, as you think about how you might define a subject and focus for your own cultural literacy paper think about which organizing strategies might help you begin drafting your paper.

Reading as a writer means paying attention to the invention and arrangement strategies other writers use and adapting them for use in your own work.

School vs. Education

Russell Baker

Russell Baker (1925–) was born in a rural town in Virginia and grew up in New Jersey and Maryland. He received his B. A. in English from Johns Hopkins University in 1947 and worked as a reporter for the Baltimore Sun *and then the* New York Times. *In 1962 he began writing his "Observer" column for the* Times, *which was syndicated in over 400 newspapers for more than two decades. His topics range from the mundane everyday annoyances to serious social problems, and his style is generally casual but thoughtful. In 1979 he received the Pulitzer Prize for distinguished commentary; he received the Prize again for his autobiography* Growing Up *(1982). His collections of columns and essays include* All Things Considered *(1965),* Poor Russell's Almanac *(1972),* So This is Depravity *(1980)* The Rescue of Miss Yaskell and Other Pipe Dreams *(1983), and* There's a Country in My Cellar *(1990). The following piece, first published in his* New York Times *column in 1975, intertwines serious commentary on American education and values with a spoof on what our schools teach. As you read it, think about the serious message Baker wants to communicate to us.*

1   B y the age of six the average child will have completed the basic American education and be ready to enter school. If the child has been attentive in these preschool years, he or she will already have mastered many skills.

From television, the child will have learned how to pick a lock, commit a fairly elaborate bank holdup, prevent wetness all day long, get the laundry twice as white, and kill people with a variety of sophisticated armaments.

From watching his parents, the child, in many cases, will already know how to smoke, how much soda to mix with whiskey, what kind of language to use when angry, and how to violate the speed laws without being caught.

At this point, the child is ready for the second stage of education, which occurs in school. There, a variety of lessons may be learned in the very first days.

5   The teacher may illustrate the economic importance of belonging to a strong union by closing down the school before the child arrives. Fathers and mothers may demonstrate to the child the social cohesion that can be built on shared hatred by demonstrating their dislike for children whose pigmentation displeases them. In the latter event, the child may receive visual instruction in techniques of stoning buses, cracking skulls with a nightstick, and subduing mobs with tear gas. Formal education has begun.

During formal education, the child learns that life is for testing. This stage lasts twelve years, a period during which the child learns that success comes from telling testers what they want to hear.

Early in this stage, the child learns that he is either dumb or smart. If the teacher puts intelligent demands upon the child, the child learns he is smart. If the teacher expects little of the child, the child learns he is dumb and soon quits bothering to tell the testers what they want to hear.

At this point, education becomes more subtle. The child taught by school that he is dumb observes that neither he, she, nor any of the many children who are even dumber, ever fails to be promoted to the next grade. From this, the child learns that while everybody talks a lot about the virtue of being smart, there is very little incentive to stop being dumb.

What is the point of school, besides attendance? the child wonders. As the end of the first formal stage of education approaches, school answers this question. The point is to equip the child to enter college.

10   Children who have been taught they are smart have no difficulty. They have been happily telling testers what they want to hear for twelve years. Being artists at telling testers what they want to hear, they

55

are admitted to college joyously, where they promptly learn that they are the hope of America.

Children whose education has been limited to adjusting themselves to their schools' low estimates of them are admitted to less joyous colleges which, in some cases, may teach them to read.

At this stage of education, a fresh question arises for everyone. If the point of lower education was to get into college, what is the point of college? The answer is soon learned. The point of college is to prepare the student—no longer a child now—to get into graduate school. In college the student learns that it is no longer enough simply to tell the testers what they want to hear. Many are tested for graduate school; few are admitted.

Those excluded may be denied valuable certificates to prosper in medicine, at the bar, in the corporate boardroom. The student learns that the race is to the cunning and often, alas, to the unprincipled.

Thus, the student learns the importance of destroying competitors and emerges richly prepared to play his role in the great simmering melodrama of American life.

15   Afterward, the former student's destiny fulfilled, his life rich with   15 Oriental carpets, rare porcelain, and full bank accounts, he may one day find himself with the leisure and the inclination to open a book with a curious mind, and start to become educated.

How We Listen to Music

Aaron Copland

Aaron Copland (1900–1990) was a well-known modern composer. Born in New York City, he studied music in New York and France. His early successes in his twenties led to a musical career that included many compositions, piano performances, teaching, and writing. His music is marked by adaptations of American folk stories, including his ballet Billy the Kid *(1939) and* John Henry *(1940). His most popular symphony is* El Salon Mexico *(1936); he also composed avant-garde compositions such as* Piano Variations *(1930). Among the several books he wrote about music is* What to Listen for in Music *(1939), from which the following essay is excerpted. Although many composers do not like to talk about what their music means or what it expresses, as Copland remarks in this essay, he believes we should try to understand music fully by paying attention to all its dimensions.*

1 We all listen to music according to our separate capacities. But, for the sake of analysis, the whole listening process may become clearer if we break it up into its component parts, so to speak. In a certain sense we all listen to music on three separate planes. For lack of a better terminology, one might name these: (1) the sensuous plane, (2) the expressive plane, (3) the sheerly musical plane. The only advantage to be gained from mechanically splitting up the listening process into these hypothetical planes is the clearer view to be had of the way in which we listen.

The simplest way of listening to music is to listen for the sheer pleasure of the musical sound itself. That is the sensuous plane. It is the plane on which we hear music without thinking, without considering it in any way. One turns on the radio while doing something else and absent-mindedly bathes in the sound. A kind of brainless but attractive state of mind is engendered by the mere sound appeal of the music.

You may be sitting in a room reading this book. Imagine one note struck on the piano. Immediately that one note is enough to change the atmosphere of the room—providing that the sound element in music is a powerful and mysterious agent, which it would be foolish to deride or belittle.

The surprising thing is that many people who consider themselves qualified music lovers abuse that plane in listening. They go to concerts in order to lose themselves. They use music as a consolation or an escape. They enter an ideal world where one doesn't have to think of the realities of everyday life. Of course they aren't thinking about the music either. Music allows them to leave it, and they go off to a place to dream, dreaming because of and apropos of the music yet never quite listening to it.

5   Yes, the sound appeal of music is a potent and primitive force, but   5
you must not allow it to usurp a disproportionate share of your interest. The sensuous plane is an important one in music, a very important one, but it does not constitute the whole story.

There is no need to digress further on the sensuous plane. Its appeal to every normal human being is self-evident. There is, however, such a thing as becoming more sensitive to the different kinds of sound stuff as used by various composers. For all composers do not use that sound stuff in the same way. Don't get the idea that the value of music is commensurate with its sensuous appeal or that the loveliest sounding music is made by the greatest composer. If that were so, Ravel would be a greater creator than Beethoven. The point is that the sound element varies with each composer, that his usage of sound forms an integral part of his style and must be taken into account when listening. The reader can see, therefore, that a more conscious approach is valuable even on this primary plane of music listening.

The second plane on which music exists is what I have called the expressive one. Here, immediately, we tread on controversial ground. Composers have a way of shying away from any discussion of music's expressive side. Did not Stravinsky himself proclaim that his music was an "object," a "thing," with a life of its own, and with no other meaning than its own purely musical existence? This intransigent attitude of Stravinsky's may be due to the fact that so many people have tried to read different meanings into so many pieces. Heaven knows it is difficult enough to say precisely what it is that a piece of music means, to say it definitely, to say it finally so that everyone is satisfied with your explanation. But that should not lead one to the other extreme of denying to music the right to be "expressive."

My own belief is that all music has an expressive power, some more and some less, but that all music has a certain meaning behind the notes and that the meaning behind the notes constitutes, after all, what the piece is saying, what the piece is about. The whole problem can be stated quite simply by asking, "Is there a meaning to music?" My answer to that would be, "Yes." And "Can you state in so many words what the meaning is?" My answer to that would be, "No." Therein lies the difficulty.

Simple-minded souls will never be satisfied with the answer to the second of these questions. They always want music to have a meaning, and the more concrete it is the better they like it. The more the music reminds them of a train, a storm, a funeral, or any other familiar conception the more expressive it appears to be to them. This popular idea of music's meaning—stimulated and abetted by the usual run of musical commentator—should be discouraged wherever and whenever it is met. One timid lady once confessed to me that she suspected something seriously lacking in her appreciation of music because of her inability to connect it with anything definite. That is getting the whole thing backward, of course.

Still, the question remains, How close should the intelligent music lover wish to come to pinning a definite meaning to any particular work? No closer than a general concept, I should say. Music expresses, at different moments, serenity or exuberance, regrets or triumph, fury or delight. It expresses each of these moods, and many others, in a numberless variety of subtle shadings and differences. It may even express a state of meaning for which there exists no adequate word in any language. In that case, musicians often like to say that it has only a purely musical meaning. They sometimes go further and say that *all* music has only a purely musical meaning. What they really mean is that no appropriate word can be found to express the music's meaning and that, even if it could, they do not feel the need of finding it.

But whatever the professional musician may hold, most musical novices still search for specific words with which to pin down their musical reactions. That is why they always find Tschaikovsky easier to "understand" than Beethoven. In the first place, it is easier to pin a meaning-word on a Tschaikovsky piece than on a Beethoven one. Much easier. Moreover, with the Russian composer, every time you come back to a piece of his it almost always says the same thing to you, whereas with Beethoven it is often quite difficult to put your finger right on what he is saying. And any musician will tell you that that is why Beethoven is the greater composer. Because music which always says the same thing to you will necessarily soon become dull music, but music whose meaning is slightly different with each hearing has a greater chance of remaining alive.

Listen, if you can, to the forty-eight fugue themes of Bach's *Well Tempered Clavichord.* Listen to each theme, one after another. You will soon realize that each theme mirrors a different world of feeling. You will also soon realize that the more beautiful a theme seems to you the harder it is to find any word that will describe it to your complete satisfaction. Yes, you will certainly know whether it is a gay theme or a sad one. You will be able, in other words, in your own mind, to draw a frame of emotional feeling around your theme. Now study the sad one a little closer. Try to pin down the exact quality of its sadness. Is it pessimistically sad or resignedly sad; is it fatefully sad or smilingly sad?

Let us suppose that you are fortunate and can describe to your own satisfaction in so many words the exact meaning of your chosen theme. There is still no guarantee that anyone else will be satisfied. Nor need they be. The important thing is that each one feel for himself the specific expressive quality of a theme or, similarly, an entire piece of music. And if it is a great work of art, don't expect it to mean exactly the same thing to you each time you return to it.

Themes or pieces need not express only one emotion, of course. Take such a theme as the first main one of the *Ninth Symphony,* for example. It is clearly made up of different elements. It does not say only one thing. Yet anyone hearing it immediately gets a feeling of strength, a feeling of power. It isn't a power that comes simply because the theme is played loudly. It is a power inherent in the theme itself. The extraordinary strength and vigor of the theme results in the listener's receiving an impression that a forceful statement has been made. But one should never try to boil it down to "the fateful hammer of life," etc. That is where the trouble begins. The musician, in his exasperation, says it means nothing but the notes themselves, whereas the nonprofessional is only too anxious to hang on to any explanation that gives him the illusion of getting closer to the music's meaning.

15   Now, perhaps, the reader will know better what I mean when I say that music does have an expressive meaning but that we cannot say in so many words what that meaning is.

The third plane on which music exists is the sheerly musical plane. Besides the pleasurable sound of music and the expressive feeling that it gives off, music does exist in terms of the notes themselves and of their manipulation. Most listeners are not sufficiently conscious of this third plane. . . .

Professional musicians, on the other hand, are, if anything, too conscious of the mere notes themselves. They often fall into the error of becoming so engrossed with their arpeggios and staccatos that they forget the deeper aspects of the music they are performing. But from the layman's standpoint, it is not so much a matter of getting over bad habits on the sheerly musical plane as of increasing one's awareness of what is going on, in so far as the notes are concerned.

When the man in the street listens to the "notes themselves" with any degree of concentration, he is most likely to make some mention of the melody. Either he hears a pretty melody or he does not, and he generally lets it go at that. Rhythm is likely to gain his attention next, particularly if it seems exciting. But harmony and tone color are generally taken for granted, if they are thought of consciously at all. As for music's having a definite form of some kind, that idea seems never to have occurred to him.

It is very important for all of us to become more alive to music on its sheerly musical plane. After all, an actual musical material is being used. The intelligent listener must be prepared to increase his awareness of the musical material and what happens to it. He must hear the melodies, the rhythms, the harmonies, the tone colors in a more conscious fashion. But above all he must, in order to follow the line of the composer's thought, know something of the principles of musical form. Listening to all of these elements is listening on the sheerly musical plane.

20   Let me repeat that I have split up mechanically the three separate planes on which we listen merely for the sake of greater clarity. Actually, we never listen on one or the other of these planes. What we do is to correlate them—listening in all three ways at the same time. It takes no mental effort, for we do it instinctively.

Perhaps an analogy with what happens to us when we visit the theater will make this instinctive correlation clearer. In the theater, you are aware of the actors and actresses, costumes and sets, sounds and movements. All these give one the sense that the theater is a pleasant place to be in. They constitute the sensuous plane in our theatrical reactions.

The expressive plane in the theater would be derived from the feeling that you get from what is happening on the stage. You are moved to pity, excitement, or gayety. It is this general feeling, generated aside from the particular words being spoken, a certain emotional something which exists on the stage, that is analogous to the expressive quality in music.

The plot and plot development is equivalent to our sheerly musical plane. The playwright creates and develops a character in just the same way that a composer creates and develops a theme. According to the degree of your awareness of the way in which the artist in either field handles his material you will become a more intelligent listener.

It is easy enough to see that the theatergoer never is conscious of any of these elements separately. He is aware of them all at the same time. The same is true of music listening. We simultaneously and without thinking listen on all three planes.

25 In a sense, the ideal listener is both inside and outside the music 25 at the same moment, judging it and enjoying it, wishing it would go one way and watching it go another—almost like the composer at the moment he composes it; because in order to write his music, the composer must also be inside and outside his music, carried away by it and yet coldly critical of it. A subjective and objective attitude is implied in both creating and listening to music.

What the reader should strive for, then, is a more *active* kind of listening. Whether you listen to Mozart or Duke Ellington, you can deepen your understanding of music only by being a more conscious and aware listener—not someone who is just listening, but someone who is listening *for* something.

The Myth of the Latin Woman: I Just Met a Girl Named María

Judith Ortiz Cofer

Judith Ortiz Cofer (1952–) was born in Hormigueros, Puerto Rico, and emigrated to the United States when she was four. Cofer attended Augusta College and Florida Atlantic University; she was also a Scholar of the English Speaking Union at Oxford University. She has worked as a bilingual teacher in the Florida public schools, and as a visiting writer at Vanderbilt University and the University of Michigan, Ann Arbor. Cofer is currently the Franklin Professor of English and Creative Writing at The University of Georgia. An award-winning poet, Cofer has received grants from the Witter Bynner Foundation and the National Endowment for the Arts. Her books include The Line of the Sun *(1989),* Silent Dancing *(1990),* The Latin Deli *(1993),* Reaching for the Mainland and Selected New Poems *(1995),* The Year of Our Revolution *(1998),* Woman In Front of the Sun: On Becoming a Writer *(2000),* A Love Story Beginning in Spanish: Poems *(2005), as well as a children's book,* Call Me Maria *(2004). Cofer, who has also written for* Glamour *and* The Kenyon Review, *often combines her love of language with her interest in the lives and traditions of Puerto Ricans. In this essay, from* The Latin Deli, *Cofer describes how her Latino ancestry attracts unpleasant stereotyping.*

1   On a bus trip to London from Oxford University where I was earning some graduate credits one summer, a young man, obviously fresh from a pub, spotted me and as if struck by

From *The Latin Deli: Prose and Poetry* by Judith Ortiz Cofer. Published by the University of Georgia Press.

inspiration went down on his knees in the aisle. With both hands over his heart he broke into an Irish tenor's rendition of "Maria" from *West Side Story*. My politely amused fellow passengers gave his lovely voice the round of gentle applause it deserved. Though I was not quite as amused, I managed my version of an English smile: no show of teeth, no extreme contortions of the facial muscles—I was at this time of my life practicing reserve and cool. Oh, that British control, how I coveted it. But "Maria" had followed me to London, reminding me of a prime fact of my life: you can leave the island, master the English language, and travel as far as you can, but if you are a Latina, especially one like me who so obviously belongs to Rita Moreno's gene pool, the island travels with you.

This is sometimes a very good thing—it may win you that extra minute of someone's attention. But with some people, the same things can make *you* an island—not a tropical paradise but an Alcatraz, a place nobody wants to visit. As a Puerto Rican girl living in the United States and wanting like most children to "belong," I resented the stereotype that my Hispanic appearance called forth from many people I met.

Growing up in a large urban center in New Jersey during the 1960s, I suffered from what I think of as "cultural schizophrenia." Our life was designed by my parents as a microcosm of their *casas* on the island. We spoke in Spanish, ate Puerto Rican food bought at the *bodega,* and practiced strict Catholicism at a church that allotted us a one-hour slot each week for mass, performed in Spanish by a Chinese priest trained as a missionary for Latin America.

As a girl I was kept under strict surveillance by my parents, since my virtue and modesty were, by their cultural equation, the same as their honor. As a teenager I was lectured constantly on how to behave as a proper *senorita.* But it was a conflicting message I received, since the Puerto Rican mothers also encouraged their daughters to look and act like women and to dress in clothes our Anglo friends and their mothers found too "mature" and flashy. The difference was, and is, cultural; yet I often felt humiliated when I appeared at an American friend's party wearing a dress more suitable to a semi-formal than to a playroom birthday celebration. At Puerto Rican festivities, neither the music nor the colors we wore could be too loud.

5   I remember Career Day in our high school, when teachers told us   5 to come dressed as if for a job interview. It quickly became obvious that to the Puerto Rican girls "dressing up" meant wearing their mother's

ornate jewelry and clothing, more appropriate (by mainstream standards) for the company Christmas party than as daily office attire. That morning I had agonized in front of my closet, trying to figure out what a "career girl" would wear. I knew how to dress for school (at the Catholic school I attended, we all wore uniforms), I knew how to dress for Sunday mass, and I knew what dresses to wear for parties at my relatives' homes. Though I do not recall the precise details of my Career Day outfit, it must have been a composite of these choices. But I remember a comment my friend (an Italian American) made in later years that coalesced my impressions of that day. She said that at the business school she was attending, the Puerto Rican girls always stood out for wearing "everything at once." She meant, of course, too much jewelry, too many accessories. On that day at school we were simply made the negative models by the nuns, who were themselves not credible fashion experts to any of us. But it was painfully obvious to me that to the others, in their tailored skirts and silk blouses, we must have seemed "hopeless" and "vulgar." Though I now know that most adolescents feel out of step much of the time, I also know that for the Puerto Rican girls of my generation that sense was intensified. The way our teachers and classmates looked at us that day in school was just a taste of the cultural clash that awaited us in the real world, where prospective employers and men on the street would often misinterpret our tight skirts and jingling bracelets as a "come-on."

Mixed cultural signals have perpetuated certain stereotypes—for example, that of the Hispanic woman as the "hot tamale" or sexual firebrand. It is a one-dimensional view that the media have found easy to promote. In their special vocabulary, advertisers have designated "sizzling" and "smoldering" as the adjectives of choice for describing not only the foods but also the women of Latin America. From conversations in my house I recall hearing about the harassment that Puerto Rican women endured in factories where the "boss-men" talked to them as if sexual innuendo was all they understood, and worse, often gave them the choice of submitting to their advances or being fired.

It is custom, however, not chromosomes, that leads us to choose scarlet over pale pink. As young girls, it was our mothers who influenced our decisions about clothes and colors—mothers who had grown up on a tropical island where the natural environment was a riot of primary colors, where showing your skin was one way to keep cool as well as to look sexy. Most important of all, on the island, women perhaps felt freer to dress and move more provocatively since, in most cases, they were protected by the traditions, mores, and laws of a Spanish/Catholic system of morality and machismo whose main rule was: *You may look at my sister, but if you touch her I will kill you.* The extended family and church structure could provide a young woman with a circle of safety in her small pueblo on the island; if a man "wronged" a girl, everyone would close in to save her family honor.

My mother has told me about dressing in her best party clothes on Saturday nights and going to the town's plaza to promenade with her girl-friends in front of the boys they liked. The males were thus given an opportunity to admire the women and to express their admiration in the form of *piropos:* erotically charged street poems they composed on the spot. (I have myself been subjected to a few *piropos* while visiting the island, and they can be outrageous, although custom dictates that they must never cross into obscenity.) This ritual, as I understand it, also entails a show of studied indifference on the woman's part; if she is "decent," she must not acknowledge the man's impassioned words. So I do understand how things can be lost in translation. When a Puerto Rican girl dressed in her idea of what is attractive meets a man from the mainstream culture who has been trained to react to certain types of clothing as a sexual signal, a clash is likely to take place. I remember the boy who took me to my first formal dance leaning over to plant a sloppy, over-eager kiss painfully on my mouth; when I didn't respond with sufficient passion, he remarked resentfully: "I thought you Latin girls were supposed to mature early," as if I were expected to *ripen* like a fruit or vegetable, not just grow into womanhood like other girls.

It is surprising to my professional friends that even today some people, including those who should know better, still put others "in their place." It happened to me most recently during a stay at a classy metropolitan hotel favored by young professional couples for weddings. Late one evening after the theater, as I walked toward my room with a colleague (a woman with whom I was coordinating an arts program), a middle-aged man in a tuxedo, with a young girl in satin and lace on his arm, stepped directly into our path. With his champagne glass extended toward me, he exclaimed "Evita!"

10   Our way blocked, my companion and I listened as the man half-   10
recited, half-bellowed "Don't Cry for Me, Argentina." When he

finished, the young girl said: "How about a round of applause for my daddy?" We complied, hoping this would bring the silly spectacle to a close. I was becoming aware that our little group was attracting the attention of the other guests. "Daddy" must have perceived this too, and he once more barred the way as we tried to walk past him. He began to shout-sing a ditty to the tune of "La Bamba"—except the lyrics were about a girl named Maria whose exploits rhymed with her name and gonorrhea. The girl kept saying "Oh, Daddy" and looking at me with pleading eyes. She wanted me to laugh along with the others. My companion and I stood silently waiting for the man to end his offensive song. When he finished, I looked not at him but at his daughter. I advised her calmly never to ask her father what he had done in the army. Then I walked between them and to my room. My friend complimented me on my cool handling of the situation, but I confessed that I had really wanted to push the jerk into the swimming pool. This same man—probably a corporate executive, well-educated, even worldly by most standards—would not have been likely to regale an Anglo woman with a dirty song in public. He might have checked his impulse by assuming that she could be somebody's wife or mother, or at least *somebody* who might take offense. But, to him, I was just an Evita or a Maria: merely a character in his cartoon-populated universe.

Another facet of the myth of the Latin woman in the United States is the menial, the domestic—Maria the housemaid or counter-girl. It's true that work as domestics, as waitresses, and in factories is all that's available to women with little English and few skills. But the myth of the Hispanic menial—the funny maid, mispronouncing words and cooking up a spicy storm in a shiny California kitchen—has been perpetuated by the media in the same way that "Mammy" from *Gone with the Wind* became America's idea of the black woman for generations. Since I do not wear my diplomas around my neck for all to see, I have on occasion been sent to that "kitchen" where some think I obviously belong.

One incident has stayed with me, though I recognize it as a minor offense. My first public poetry reading took place in Miami, at a restaurant where a luncheon was being held before the event. I was nervous and excited as I walked in with notebook in hand. An older woman motioned me to her table, and thinking (foolish me) that she wanted me to autograph a copy of my newly published slender volume of verse, I went over. She ordered a cup of coffee from me, assuming that I was the waitress. (Easy enough to mistake my poems for menus, I suppose.) I know it wasn't an intentional act of cruelty. Yet of all the good things that happened later, I remember that scene most clearly, because it reminded me of what I had to overcome before anyone would take me seriously. In retrospect I understand that my anger gave my reading fire. In fact, I have almost always taken any doubt in my abilities as a challenge, the result most often being the satisfaction of winning a convert, of seeing the cold, appraising eyes warm to my words, the body language change, the smile that indicates I have opened some avenue for communication. So that day as I read, I looked directly at that woman. Her lowered eyes told me she was embarrassed at her faux pas, and when I willed her to look up at me, she graciously allowed me to punish her with my full attention. We shook hands at the end of the reading and I never saw her again. She has probably forgotten the entire incident, but maybe not.

Yet I am one of the lucky ones. There are thousands of Latinas without the privilege of an education or the entrees into society that I have. For them life is a constant struggle against the misconceptions perpetuated by the myth of the Latina. My goal is to try to replace the old stereotypes with a much more interesting set of realities. Every time I give a reading, I hope the stories I tell, the dreams and fears I examine in my work, can achieve some universal truth that will get my audience past the particulars of my skin color, my accent, or my clothes.

I once wrote a poem in which I called all Latinas "God's brown daughters." This poem is really a prayer of sorts, offered upward, but also, through the human-to-human channel of art, outward. It is a prayer for communication and for respect. In it, Latin women pray "in Spanish to an Anglo God/with a Jewish heritage," and they are "fervently hoping/that if not omnipotent,/at least He be bilingual."

The Merits of Meritocracy
David Brooks

David Brooks (1961–) is best known for his sharp and witty conservative commentary on public television's News Hour *with Jim Lehrer. Brooks graduated from the University of Chicago with a degree in history. He turned to writing political and social commentary and is now a leading commentator on PBS, CNN, and National Public Radio. He writes for* Newsweek *where he is a contributing editor, as well as for the* New York Times. *He is also a senior editor at the* Weekly Standard. *An anthology of his essays and commentaries is titled* Backward and Upward: The New Conservative Writing *(1996). His books include* Bobos in Paradise: The New Upper Class and How They Got There *(2000) and* On Paradise Drive: How We Live Now (and Always Have) *(2004).*

Children of the privileged must work very hard for what they have and for what they will get. Brooks uses the example of his daughter to show how busy she is and how she will have to compete to get into a great school and to find a greater job after school.

My daughter is a four-helmet kid. She has a regular helmet she wears bike riding, pogo sticking, and when she borrows her older brother's skateboard. She has a pink batting helmet, which she wears during her Little League baseball games. She has a helmet for horseback-riding lessons, on Sundays. And she has a helmet for ice hockey, which she plays on Friday afternoons. (For hockey she also has an equipment bag large enough to hold several corpses.) My daughter's not even a jock (although she is something of a live wire). Her main interest is art, which she does in an after-school program on Tuesdays and at home on her own.

But it's her helmets that really got me thinking. They're generally scattered around the equipment racks in our garage, along with her brothers' helmet collections and all manner of sleds, mitts, scooters, bicycles, and balls, and they represent a certain sort of childhood— a childhood that has now become typical in middle-class America.

It's a busy childhood, filled with opportunities, activities, teams, coaches, and, inevitably, gear. It's a safety-conscious childhood, with ample adult supervision. And it is, I believe (at least I want to believe), a happy and fulfilling childhood that will prepare my daughter for a happy adult life.

This sort of childhood is different from the childhoods Americans have traditionally had. It's not an independent childhood, like Huck Finn's or the Bowery Boys'. Today's middle-class kids, by and large, don't live apart from adult society, free to explore and experiment and, through adventure and misadventure, teach themselves the important lessons of life. Nor is it a Horatio Alger childhood. Middle-class kids by definition haven't come from poverty and deprivation. Nor do they build self-discipline from having to work on a farm. If they hunger for success, it's not because they started at the bottom.

5   Today's mode of raising kids generates a lot of hand-wringing and anxiety, some of it on my part. We fear that kids are spoiled by the abundance and frenetic activity all around them. We fear that the world of suburban sprawl, Game Boys, Britney Spears CDs, and shopping malls will dull their moral senses. We fear that they are too deferential to authority, or that they are confronted with so many choices that they never have to make real commitments. Or we fear that they are skipping over childhood itself. The toy companies call this phenomenon "age compression": Kids who are ten no longer want toys that used to appeal to ten-year-olds. Now it is three-to-five-year-olds who go for Barbie dolls. By the time a girl is seven she wants to be a mini-adult.

But I've come to believe that our fears are overblown. The problem is that the way kids (and, for that matter, the rest of us) live is estranged from the formulaic ideas we have about building character. We assume that character is forged through hardship—economic deprivation, war, and so on—and that we who have had it easy, who have grown up in this past half century of peace and prosperity, must necessarily have weak or suspect souls.

It's true that we live amid plenty; even in time of war we are told to keep shopping. But today's kids have a way of life that entails its own character-building process, its own ethical system. They live in a world of almost crystalline meritocracy. Starting at birth, middle-class Americans are called on to master skills, do well in school, practice sports, excel in extracurricular activities, get into college, build their résumés, change careers, be good in bed, set up retirement plans, and so on. This is a way of life that emphasizes individual achievement, self-propulsion, perpetual improvement, and permanent exertion.

The prime ethical imperative for the meritocrat is self-fulfillment. The phrase sounds New Agey; it calls to mind a Zen vegan sitting on the beach at dawn contemplating his narcissism. But over the past several years the philosophers Charles Taylor, of McGill University, and Alan Gewirth, of the University of Chicago, have argued that a serious moral force is contained in the idea of self-ful fillment. Meritocrats may not necessarily be able to articulate this morality, but they live by it nonetheless.

It starts with the notion that we have a lifelong mission to realize our capacities. "It is a bringing of oneself to flourishing completion, an unfolding of what is strongest or best in oneself, so that it represents the successful culmination of one's aspirations or potentialities," Gewirth wrote in *Self-Fulfillment* (1998). The way we realize our potential is through our activities. By ceaselessly striving to improve at the things we enjoy, we come to define, enlarge, and attain our best selves. These activities are the bricks of our identities; if we didn't write or play baseball or cook or litigate (or whatever it is we do well), we would cease to be who we are. This is what Karl Marx was describing when he wrote, "Milton produced *Paradise Lost* as a silkworm produces silk, as the activation of his own nature."

10   In this mode of living, character isn't something one forges as a   10 youth and then retains thereafter. Morality doesn't come to one in a single revelation or a grand moment of epiphany. Instead, virtue and character are achieved gradually and must be maintained through a relentless struggle for self-improvement. We are in an ongoing dialogue with our inadequacies, and we are happiest when we are most deeply engaged in overcoming them.

This is not a solitary process. Once ensconced in an activity, we find ourselves surrounded by mentors, coaches, teachers, colleagues, teammates, consultants, readers, and audience members. Society helps us in two ways. First, it gives us opportunities to participate in the things that will allow us to realize our capacities: Parents earnestly cast about for activities their children will love, and then spend their weekends driving them from one to another. Good schools have extracurricular offerings. Good companies and organizations allow their employees and members to explore new skills, and great nations have open, fluid societies—so that individuals can find their best avenues and go as far as their merit allows.

Second, society surrounds the individual with a web of instruction, encouragement, and recognition. The hunger for recognition is a great motivator for the meritocrat. People define themselves in part by the extent to which others praise and appreciate them. In traditional societies recognition was determined by birth, breeding, and social station, but in a purified meritocracy people have to win it through performance. Each person responds to signals from those around him, working hard at activities that win praise and abandoning those that don't. (America no doubt leads the world in trophy production per capita.) An individual's growth, then, is a joint project of the self and society.

In this joint project individuals not only improve their capacities; they also come to realize that they cannot fully succeed unless they make a contribution to the society that helped to shape them. A scientist may be good at science, but she won't feel fulfilled unless she has made important discoveries or innovations that help those around her. Few meritocrats are content to master pointless tasks.

Social contributions—giving back—flow easily and naturally from the meritocrat's life mission. Baseball players enjoy clinics where they share tips with younger players. Parents devote many hours to coaching, or they become teachers, managers, and mentors. In the best relationships what follows is a sort of love affair. Mentor and pupil work hard to help each other and to honor each other's effort. Most find that they glimpse their best selves while working with others on an arduous undertaking, whether it is staging a play, competing for a championship, or arguing a case in court.

15 The great moral contest for the meritocrat is not between good 15 and evil or virtue and vice. Most meritocrats are prudent, so they

Cultural Literacy Resources from T.E.D.com

Schools Kill Creativity by Ken Robinson
The Worlds English Mania by Jay Walker
Endangered Cultures by Wade Davis

Disciplinary Literacies

Disciplinary Literacies: Introduction

The readings we selected for this section serve three major purposes. First, they are meant to familiarize you with some of the ways that people think about writing, reading, and researching as literacy activities that require flexible strategies that allow us to respond to lots of different literacy events effectively. Second, they offer even more invention and arrangement strategies for you to identify and use as appropriate in your own papers. Third, these readings give you a chance to focus on revision as an activity that changes something outside of the text itself.

As you think about how you might focus your own exploration of a disciplinary form of literacy, try to identify what will change as a result of the information you gather. For example, as William Diehl and Larry Mikulecky gather information about how people read and write at work, they revise the idea that school educates people to meet the literacy expectations in most workplaces. As Larry Haun narrates the story of a carpenter's life, he revises the idea that there is no connection between larger cultural changes in technology and material needs and the life of individual workers. What will your exploration of disciplinary literacy revise? For what audience? How?

Thinking about invention and arrangement, and asking questions about the revisionary purpose of your writing processes helps you read as a writer and write with the needs of your readers in mind.

Winning Hearts and Minds in War on Plagiarism

Scott Jaschik

Scott Jaschik grew up in Rochester, New York and graduated from Cornell University in 1985. His articles have appeared in numerous publications, such as The New York Times, The Washington Post, The Boston Globe, Campus Watch, *and* Salon. *From 1999 to 2003 he was an editor for* The Chronicle of Higher Education. *Jaschik is a co-founder of* Inside Higher Ed, *an online source for news, commentary, and jobs pertaining to higher education. He is a mentor in the community college fellowship program for the Hechinger Institute on Education and Media. He has received honors for his reporting from* The Washington Monthly *and from Investigative Reporters and Editors, a non-profit organization dedicated to improving the quality of investigative reporting. Jaschik currently lives in Washington, DC. In the following article from* Inside Higher Ed, *he profiles one professor's unique approach to teaching students about plagiarism and how to avoid it.*

1   It's come to this: Writing professors are so desperate for new ways to teach undergraduates about academic integrity that they are assigning them to plagiarize.

That's what Kate Hagopian, an instructor in the first-year writing program at North Carolina State University, does. For one assignment, she gives her students a short writing passage and then a prompt for a standard student short essay. She asks her students to turn in two versions. In one they are told that they must plagiarize. In the second, they

Reprinted by permission from *Inside Higher Ed*, April 7, 2008.

are told not to. The prior night, the students were given an online tutorial on plagiarism and Hagopian said she has become skeptical that having the students "parrot back what we've told them" accomplishes anything. Her hope is that this unusual assignment might change that.

After the students turn in their two responses to the essay prompt, Hagopian shares some with the class. Not surprisingly, the students do know how to plagiarize—but were uncomfortable admitting as much. Hagopian said that the assignment is always greeted with "uncomfortable laughter" as the students must pretend that they never would have thought of plagiarizing on their own. Given the right to do so, they turn in essays with many direct quotes without attribution. Of course in their essays that are supposed to be done without plagiarism, she still finds problems—not so much with passages repeated verbatim, but with paraphrasing or using syntax in ways that were so similar to the original that they required attribution.

When she started giving the assignment, she sort of hoped, Hagopian said, to see students turn in "nuanced tricky demonstrations" of plagiarism, but she mostly gets garden variety copying. But what she is doing is having detailed conversations with her students about what is and isn't plagiarism—and by turning everyone into a plagiarist (at least temporarily), she makes the conversation something that can take place openly.

5 "Students know I am listening," she said. And by having the conversation in this way—as opposed to reading the riot act—she said she is demonstrating that all plagiarism is not the same, whether in technique, motivation or level of sophistication. There is a difference between "deliberate fraud" and "failed apprenticeship," she said.

Hagopian's approach was among many described at various sessions last week at the *annual meeting of the Conference of College Composition and Communication,* in New Orleans. Writing instructors—especially those tasked with teaching freshmen—are very much on the front lines of the war against plagiarism. As much as other faculty members, they resent plagiarism by their students—and in fact several of the talks featured frank discussion of how betrayed writing instructors feel when someone turns in plagiarized work.

That anger does motivate some to use the software that detects plagiarism as part of an effort to scare students and weed out plagiarists, and there was some discussion along those lines. But by and large, the instructors at the meeting said that they didn't have any confidence that these services were attacking the roots of the problem or finding all of the plagiarism. Several people quipped that if the software really detected all plagiarism, plenty of campuses would be unable to hold classes, what with all of the sessions needed for academic integrity boards.

While there was a group therapy element to some of the discussions, there was also a strong focus on trying new solutions. Freshmen writing instructors after all don't have the option available to other faculty members of just blaming the problem on the failures of those who teach first-year comp.

What to do? New books being displayed in the exhibit hall included several trying to shift the plagiarism debate beyond a matter of pure enforcement. Among them were *Originality, Imitation, and Plagiarism: Teaching Writing in the Digital Age,* just published by the University of Michigan (and *profiled on Inside Higher Ed*), and *Pluralizing Plagiarism: Identities, Contexts, Pedagogies,* released in February by Boynton/Cook.

10   Like Hagopian, many of those at the meeting said that they are   10 focused on trying to better understand their students, what makes them plagiarize, and what might make them better understand academic integrity. There wasn't much talk of magic bullets, but lots of ideas about ways to better see the issue from a student perspective— and to find ways to use that perspective to promote integrity.

What Students Are Saying

Roy Stamper, associate director of the writing program at N.C. State, gave a presentation about a discussion he followed (for purposes of understanding, not enforcement) on *the Wolf Web,* a student discussion board. Students at N.C. State post anonymously, and while Stamper said he didn't know if all of the students were posting with accuracy about their situations, he still found plenty of truth in what they had to say.

The discussion was kicked off by a student asking for advice about certain term paper companies and whether they sold good work. The student, apparently fearful of how this would make him look, talked about how he was "completely and utterly fried and overloaded" and didn't have enough time. But he also said he didn't want to get caught plagiarizing.

While some of the responses rated various term paper sites, there was also a strong, intense reaction from other students—much of it critical. "The less time you spend posting on here the more time u get to work on your paper," wrote one student. Another student wrote: "It's called college. Grow up and get your shit done."

As other students joined in, offering suggestions on time management, Stamper said he was struck that the argument being put forth against plagiarism wasn't honesty, but efficiency, and that has its dangers too, as was brought home to him by this posting: "I say that if you can get away with doing 30 minutes worth of plagiarism as opposed to a few days of work . . . then you my friend are efficient, and not necessarily a bad person."

Yet another student argued that term paper mills could promote efficiency without turning one into a plagiarist. This student said that he used term papers obtained online to gain ideas, but that because he then rewrites these ideas himself, it's not plagiarism. "My work, with a little help," is how he characterized it.

This prompted an angry outcry from another student, who wrote: "This shit is plagiarism by any definition. If you were caught and turned over to the office of student conduct, your ass would be nailed to the cross."

Stamper said that he shared the anger of that final student (if not the idea that the plagiarist deserved to be compared to Jesus), but that once he got past the anger, he found that his lurking online raised many questions. For instance, Stamper said that while he does not believe being overworked justifies plagiarism, he has found himself wondering about whether an intense workload puts an emphasis for students on efficiency as opposed to quality. "Good writing takes a lot of time and thought. I'm not sure I'm always giving them enough time," he said.

The other thing that the online discussion demonstrated, he said, was that many students do have a strong sense of right and wrong when it comes to plagiarism and the idea that every student born in the last 30 years believes everything online is fair to use is a stereotype. Students clearly are educable, he said, and perhaps the best approach may be peer pressure—the plagiarists on the N.C. State site were clearly embarrassed and looked to justify themselves. Should writing instructors be looking to peer teaching—and specifically peer pressure—as a new tool to promote integrity, Stamper asked.

"Patchwriting" vs. Plagiarism

Several of the speakers discussed ideas related to differentiating plagiarism of the sort that involves buying a term paper or submitting another student's work with more common, and not always intentional, writing behaviors used by many students that meet textbook definitions of plagiarism but that may raise different moral and educational issues. Many cite the work of Rebecca Moore Howard (co-editor of one of the new books on plagiarism and a contributor to another), who is an associate professor of writing and rhetoric at Syracuse University.

Howard talks about "patchwriting" as a common undergraduate technique of grouping together various sources of information, frequently with only minor changes in wording and without appropriate attribution. For her own classes, she uses *a policy* that says such writing will generally lead to a poor grade, but not to sanctions that would go to someone who bought a term paper.

Along these lines, R. Gerald Nelms, an associate professor of composition and rhetoric at Southern Illinois University at Carbondale, spoke of how plagiarism must be seen as "an educational problem that requires an educational response." Much student plagiarism, he said, is unintentional, as students don't know how to take notes, how to summarize ideas, how to attribute ideas or quotes, and what paraphrasing means (and doesn't) with regard to plagiarism.

In a handout, Nelms wrote that patchwriting is "developmental plagiarism," or "behavior that is caused by the effort of the writer not fully integrated into the community for which she or he is trying to write to imitate the behavior of that community." Such plagiarism, he said, shouldn't be viewed as acceptable, but also shouldn't draw punishment. Students who engage in patchwriting need to be taught, he said, not brought up on charges. Nelms recommended a series of teaching subjects for instructors trying to show students how to write original work.

Students need to be taught to take notes, he said in his handout—so notes aren't just direct quotes or synopses, but also include students' reactions or potential use of information. In this way, students are starting to learn how to use information, not just how to repackage it. Similarly, he said in the handout, "integration involves more than citation," and must include efforts to show students how to mix various sources, how to attribute, and how to include original ideas.

"Restorative Justice" for Plagiarists

Christy Zink, an assistant professor of writing at George Washington University, used the controversy over the play *Frozen* to teach her first-year students about plagiarism. The play—about a psychiatrist who examines serial killers—was a Broadway hit, but also led to *charges of plagiarism* against its author by a psychiatrist who said that writings about her career were used without her permission for the drama.

Zink is an advocate of using "restorative justice" to deal with plagiarism. *"Restorative justice"* is an approach to criminal behavior that involves repairing the harm done by an act, but not focusing on punishment for the sake of punishment.

One of Zink's students—even though the course was focused on a discussion of plagiarism issues—plagiarized her work for an assignment. Zink said she was a bit stunned that in such a context, a student would engage in blatant plagiarism (she stressed that this wasn't a borderline case). But the student appealed to Zink's commitment to restorative justice, and said "isn't that why I'm here? To learn from my mistakes?"

While Zink worked out a punishment herself with the student—involving new work and a grade punishment—she also decided to try to apply the restorative justice ideal to the situation by talking to all three sections of the class about the situation (without identifying the student) and seeking their views on what to do. Zink's announcement to her clases that "we have a plagiarist among us" prompted a range of reactions from students.

Zink said that her students were angry at first, but that they then argued that many other considerations should go into consideration of sanctions. To most students, "intentionality matters," Zink said. Students wanted to know if the plagiarism was "an honest mistake" or deliberate. At the same time, given that the class was so focused on plagiarism, the students were doubtful that the student couldn't have known what she was doing was wrong. So the students were both interested in motivation, and not willing to accept any excuse.

The lesson, Zink said, is that while "we need the law," we also need to make decisions on more than just legalistic approaches. As another example, she described very much not wanting to like the play *Frozen,* in part because of the plagiarism issues. But she found herself deeply moved nonetheless.

An Unusual Sort-of Plagiarized Essay About Plagiarism

30 Catherine Savini, director of the Undergraduate Writing Center at 30 Columbia University, described using an unusual essay to prod students to think in new ways. The essay, *"The Ecstasy of Influence: A Plagiarism,"* appeared in *Harper's* last year. In the work, Jonathan Lethem makes an impassioned plea against traditional concepts of copyright and plagiarism, and he does so with words and phrases that are almost entirely plagiarized—with no credit while making the argument, but a key at the end fessing up to his writing thefts. His technique drew attention and controversy.

Even Lawrence Lessig, the Stanford University law professor who is a prominent critic of copyright restrictions, wrote in to express his discomfort at finding one of his own sentences used in the essay. "The freedom that Lethem depends upon—the freedom to integrate and build upon the work of others—does not need the license the plagiarist takes," Lessig wrote in a letter to the magazine. "The rules against plagiarism, after all, require only that words borrowed be acknowledged as borrowed." (Lessig also applauded the essay's creativity and expressed hope that it would prompt further thought by those who seek to regulate the use of others' works.)

Savini said that this text is at once "dangerous" and provocative for students because it appears to glorify plagiarism and yet goes so far—and copies the work of such noted authors—that students are taken aback. "Is it a model? Is it fodder?"

When she assigned students to write about the essay, many were afraid of a plagiarism trap. "How do I cite Lethem?" was the question she received from many students, anxious about whether citations should go to Lethem, to those whose works he borrowed, both or neither. Students were so puzzled by the situation, Savini said, that many went to unusual lengths to avoid quoting from the essay they were writing about.

Then Savini told the students she wanted them to consider sharing their writing with Lethem. This further challenged students, she said, because they normally don't think about audience in writing, placing their instructors in some other category. Thinking about people as being affected by their writing was another step in viewing writing as more than completing an assignment, Savini said, but as something with ethical issues involved. "It's a difficult leap of the imagination" for many students to think about anyone other than their instructors reading their work, but they need to, she said.

35   "Suddenly, students were asking questions without easy answers," 35 Savini said, about fairness, about the obligations of authors, and the relationship between authors and readers. "It's a morass I want my students to be in," she said.

Learning the Language

Perri Klass

Perri Klass (1958–) was born to American parents in Trinidad and earned her M. D. from Harvard in 1986, going on to become a pediatrician. She has been writing and publishing widely while pursuing her medical career. Her fiction includes two novels, Recombinations *(1985) and* Other Women's Children *(1990), and a collection of short stories,* I Am Having an Adventure *(1986). She published a collection of autobiographical essays,* A Not Entirely Benign Procedure *(1987) about her experience in medical school. The following selection, "Learning the Language," is excerpted from that book. Klass is sensitive to uses of language and understands how language affects thinking. As you read this essay, think about other special groups who also use language in unique ways.*

1   "Mrs. Tolstoy is your basic LOL in NAD, admitted for a soft rule-out MI," the intern announces. I scribble that on my patient list. In other words, Mrs. Tolstoy is a Little Old Lady in No Apparent Distress who is in the hospital to make sure she hasn't had a heart attack (rule out a Myocardial Infarction). And we think it's unlikely that she has had a heart attack (a *soft* rule-out).

If I learned nothing else during my first three months of working in the hospital as a medical student, I learned endless jargon and abbreviations. I started out in a state of primeval innocence, in which I didn't even know that "s̄ CP, SOB, N/V" meant "without chest pain, shortness of breath, or nausea and vomiting." By the end I took the abbreviations so much for granted that I would complain to my

---

Reprinted from *Not an Entirely Benign Procedure,* by permission of Elaine Markson Literary Agency. Copyright © 1987 by Perri Klass.

mother the English professor, "And can you believe I had to put down three NG tubes last night?"

"You'll have to tell me what an NG tube is if you want me to sympathize properly," my mother said. NG, nasogastric—isn't it obvious?

I picked up not only the specific expressions but also the patterns of speech and the grammatical conventions; for example, you never say that a patient's blood pressure fell or that his cardiac enzymes rose. Instead, the patient is always the subject of the verb: "He dropped his pressure." "He bumped his enzymes." This sort of construction probably reflects the profound irritation of the intern when the nurses come in the middle of the night to say that Mr. Dickinson has disturbingly low blood pressure. "Oh, he's gonna hurt me bad tonight," the intern might say, inevitably angry at Mr. Dickinson for dropping his pressure and creating a problem.

5   When chemotherapy fails to cure Mrs. Bacon's cancer, what we say is, "Mrs. Bacon failed chemotherapy."   5

"Well, we've already had one hit today, and we're up next, but at least we've got mostly stable players on our team." This means that our team (group of doctors and medical students) has already gotten one new admission today, and it is our turn again, so we'll get whoever is admitted next in emergency, but at least most of the patients we already have are fairly stable, that is, unlikely to drop their pressures or in any other way get suddenly sicker and hurt us bad. Baseball metaphor is pervasive. A no-hitter is a night without any new admissions. A player is always a patient—a nitrate player is a patient on nitrates, a unit player is a patient in the intensive care unit, and so on, until you reach the terminal player.

It is interesting to consider what it means to be winning, or doing well, in this perennial baseball game. When the intern hangs up the phone and announces, "I got a hit," that is not cause for congratulations. The team is not scoring points; rather, it is getting hit, being bombarded with new patients. The object of the game from the point of view of the doctors, considering the players for whom they are already responsible, is to get as few new hits as possible.

This special language contributes to a sense of closeness and professional spirit among people who are under a great deal of stress. As a medical student, I found it exciting to discover that I'd finally cracked the code, that I could understand what doctors said and wrote, and could use the same formulations myself. Some people seem to become enamored of the jargon for its own sake, perhaps because they are so deeply thrilled with the idea of medicine, with the idea of themselves as doctors.

I knew a medical student who was referred to by the interns on the team as Mr. Eponym because he was so infatuated with eponymous terminology, the more obscure the better. He never said "capillary pulsations" if he could say "Quincke's pulses." He would lovingly tell over the multinamed syndromes—Wolff-Parkinson-White, Lown-Ganong-Levine, Schönlein-Henoch—until the temptation to suggest Schleswig-Holstein or Stevenson-Kefauver or Baskin-Robbins became irresistible to his less reverent colleagues.

10   And there is the jargon that you don't ever want to hear yourself   10
using. You know that your training is changing you, but there are certain changes you think would be going a little too far.

The resident was describing a man with devastating terminal pancreatic cancer. "Basically he's CTD," the resident concluded. I reminded myself that I had resolved not to be shy about asking when I didn't understand things. "CTD?" I asked timidly.

The resident smirked at me. "Circling The Drain."

The images are vivid and terrible. "What happened to Mrs. Melville?"

"Oh, she boxed last night." To box is to die, of course.

15   Then there are the more pompous locutions that can make the   15
beginning medical student nervous about the effects of medical training. A friend of mine was told by his resident, "A pregnant woman with sickle-cell represents a failure of genetic counseling."

Mr. Eponym, who tried hard to talk like the doctors, once explained to me, "An infant is basically a brainstem preparation." The term "brainstem preparation," as used in neurological research, refers to an animal whose higher brain functions have been destroyed so that only the most primitive reflexes remain, like the sucking reflex, the startle reflex, and the rooting reflex.

And yet at other times the harshness dissipates into a strangely elusive euphemism. "As you know, this is a not entirely benign procedure," some doctor will say, and that will be understood to imply agony, risk of complications, and maybe even a significant mortality rate.

The more extreme forms aside, one most important function of medical jargon is to help doctors maintain some distance from their patients. By reformulating a patient's pain and problems into a language that the patient doesn't even speak, I suppose we are in some sense taking those pains and problems under our jurisdiction and also reducing their emotional impact. This linguistic separation between doctors and patients allows conversations to go on at the bedside that are unintelligible to the patient. "Naturally, we're worried about adeno-CA," the intern can say to the medical student, and lung cancer need never be mentioned.

I learned a new language this past summer. At times it thrills me to hear myself using it. It enables me to understand my colleagues, to communicate effectively in the hospital. Yet I am uncomfortably aware that I will never again notice the peculiarities and even atrocities of medical language as keenly as I did this summer. There may be specific expressions I manage to avoid, but even as I remark them, promising myself I will never use them, I find that this language is becoming my professional speech. It no longer sounds strange in my ears—or coming from my mouth. And I am afraid that as with any new language, to use it properly you must absorb not only the vocabulary but also the structure, the logic, the attitudes. At first you may notice these new and alien assumptions every time you put together a sentence, but with time and increased fluency you stop being aware of them at all. And as you lose that awareness, for better or for worse, you move closer and closer to being a doctor instead of just talking like one.

Disciplinary Literacies

Creativity and Play by Tim Brown
How Ideas Trump Crisis by Alex Tarbarrok

Remixing/
Technological
Literacies

Remixing/Technological Literacies

The readings in this section explore the ways that we communicate with things other than essays and common words. Music, visuals, video, multimodal blogs and instant messaging all offer ways to expand our audiences and exercise other forms of creativity.

As you read these essays, keep thinking about invention, arrangement, and revision, but also think about delivery. As you and your class discuss possible topics and media for your remix assignment, think about what sorts of messages, information and insights from your previous work might be best shared with others in a new media. Why share that information? Why in that medium? Thinking about delivery also pushes you to consider how to get the final project delivered to your audience. Will you need an electronic delivery system for an audience far away from your geographic location? Can you create material artifacts like paintings or write and put on a play and invite your audience to your classroom for a show?

Thinking about delivery raises all kinds of good opportunities for discussions about audience, resources, and how to make decisions about what messages are best communicated in what types of media.

For Some, the Blogging Never Stops

Katie Hafner and Tim Gnatek

Katie Hafner has a degree in German literature from the University of California, San Diego and a degree in journalism from Columbia University. She is currently a technology reporter for The New York Times *and a contributing editor for* Newsweek. *She has also published articles in* Business Week, Esquire, The New Republic, The New York Times Magazine, Wired, *and* Working Woman. *She has written four books:* Cyberpunk: Outlaws and Hackers on the Computer Frontier *(co-author, 1991);* The House at the Bridge: A Story of Modern Germany *(1995);* Where Wizards Stay Up Late: The Origins of the Internet *(co-author, 1996); and* The Well: A Story of Love, Death & Real Life in the Seminal Online Community *(2001). She lives in Marin County, California. Tim Gnatek, who contributed reporting for the following selection, has a degree in journalism from Columbia University and in 2003 and 2004 won the* Wired Magazine Award for New Media Journalism.

1   To celebrate four years of marriage, Richard Wiggins and his wife, Judy Matthews, recently spent a week in Key West, Fla. Early on the morning of their anniversary, Ms. Matthews heard her husband get up and go into the bathroom. He stayed there for a long time.

"I didn't hear any water running, so I wondered what was going on," Ms. Matthews said. When she knocked on the door, she found him seated with his laptop balanced on his knees, typing into his Web log, a collection of observations about the technical world, over a wireless link.

Blogging is a pastime for many, even a livelihood for a few. For some, it becomes an obsession. Such bloggers often feel compelled to write several times daily and feel anxious if they don't keep up. As they spend more time hunkered over their computers, they neglect family, friends and jobs. They blog at home, at work and on the road. They blog openly or sometimes, like Mr. Wiggins, quietly so as not to call attention to their habit.

"It seems as if his laptop is glued to his legs 24/7," Ms. Matthews said of her husband.

5   The number of bloggers has grown quickly, thanks to sites like   5
blogger.com, which makes it easy to set up a blog. Technorati, a blog-tracking service, has counted some 2.5 million blogs.

Of course, most of those millions are abandoned or, at best, maintained infrequently. For many bloggers, the novelty soon wears off and their persistence fades.

Sometimes, too, the realization that no one is reading sets in. A few blogs have thousands of readers, but never have so many people written so much to be read by so few. By Jupiter Research's estimate, only 4 percent of online users read blogs.

Indeed, if a blog is likened to a conversation between a writer and readers, bloggers like Mr. Wiggins are having conversations largely with themselves.

Mr. Wiggins, 48, a senior information technologist at Michigan State University in East Lansing, does not know how many readers he has; he suspects it's not many. But that does not seem to bother him.

10   "I'm just getting something off my chest," he said.   10

Nor is he deterred by the fact that he toils for hours at a time on his blog for no money. He gets satisfaction in other ways. "Sometimes there's an 'I told you so' aspect to it," he said. Recent ruminations on wigblog.blogspot.com have focused on Gmail, Google's new e-mail service. Mr. Wiggins points with pride to Wigblog posts that voiced early privacy concerns about Gmail.

Perhaps a chronically small audience is a blessing. For it seems that the more popular a blog becomes, the more some bloggers feel the need to post.

Tony Pierce started his blog three years ago while in search of a distraction after breaking up with a girlfriend. "In three years, I don't think I've missed a day," he said. Now Mr. Pierce's blog (www.tonypierce.com/blog/bloggy.htm), a chatty diary of Hollywood, writing and women in which truth sometimes mingles with fiction, averages 1,000 visitors a day.

Where some frequent bloggers might label themselves merely ardent, Mr. Pierce is more realistic. "I wouldn't call it dedicated, I would call it a problem," he said. "If this were beer, I'd be an alcoholic."

15   Mr. Pierce, who lives in Hollywood and works as a scheduler in   15 the entertainment industry, said blogging began to feel like an addiction when he noticed that he would rather be with his computer than with his girlfriend—for technical reasons.

"She's got an iMac, and I don't like her computer," Mr. Pierce said. When he is at his girlfriend's house, he feels "antsy." "We have little fights because I want to go home and write my thing," he said.

Mr. Pierce described the rush he gets from what he called "the fix" provided by his blog. "The pleasure response is twofold," he said. "You can have instant gratification; you're going to hear about something really good or bad instantly. And if I feel like I've written something good, it's enjoyable to go back and read it."

"And," he said, "like most addictions, those feelings go away quickly. So I have to do it again and again."

Joseph Lorenzo Hall, 26, a graduate student at the School of Information Management and Systems at the University of California at Berkeley who has studied bloggers, said that for some people blogging has supplanted e-mail as a way to procrastinate at work.

20   People like Mr. Pierce, who devote much of their free time to the   20 care and feeding of their own blogs and posting to other blogs, do so largely because it makes them feel productive even if it is not a paying job.

The procrastination, said Scott Lederer, 31, a fellow graduate student with Mr. Hall, has a collective feel to it. "You feel like you're participating in something important, because we're all doing it together," he said.

Jeff Jarvis, president of Advance.net, a company that builds Web sites for newspapers and magazines, and a blogging enthusiast, defended what he called one's "obligation to the blog."

"The addictive part is not so much extreme narcissism," Mr. Jarvis said. "It's that you're involved in a conversation. You have a connection to people through the blog."

Some compulsive bloggers take their obligation to extremes, blogging at the expense of more financially rewarding tasks.

25 Mr. Wiggins has missed deadline after deadline at Searcher, an 25
online periodical for which he is a paid contributor.

Barbara Quint, the editor of the magazine, said she did all she
could to get him to deliver his columns on time. Then she discovered
that Mr. Wiggins was busily posting articles to his blog instead of send-
ing her the ones he had promised, she said. "Here he is working all
night on something read by five second cousins and a dog, and I'm willing to pay him," she said.

Ms. Quint has grown more understanding of his reasons, if not
entirely sympathetic. "The Web's illusion of immortality is sometimes
more attractive than actual cash," she said.

Jocelyn Wang, a 27-year-old marketing manager in Los Angeles,
started her blog, a chronicle of whatever happens to pop into her
head (www.jozjozjoz.com), 18 months ago as an outlet for boredom.

Now she spends at least four hours a day posting to her blog and
reading other blogs. Ms. Wang's online journal is now her life. And the
people she has met through the blog are a large part of her core of friends.

30 "There is no real separation in my life," she said. Like Mr. Wiggins, 30
Ms. Wang blogs while on vacation. She stays on floors at the Hotel
Nikko in San Francisco with access to a free Internet connection. ("So I
can blog," she explains.)

Blogging for a cause can take on a special urgency. Richard Khoe, a
political consultant in Washington who in his spare time helps run a
pro-John Kerry group called Run Against Bush, posts constantly to the
blog embedded in the group's Web site (www.runagainstbush.org). He
blogs late into the night, although he knows that the site still attracts
relatively few visitors.

"Sometimes you get really particular with the kind of link you
want, so you search a little more, then a little more, then you want to
see what other people are saying about that link you chose," he said.
"And before you know it, some real time has passed."

Others find they are distracted to the point of neglectfulness.
Tom Lewis, 35, a project manager for a software firm in western
Massachusetts who has a photo blog (tomdog.buzznet.com/user), has
occasionally shown up "considerably late" for events and has put off
more than a few work-related calls to tend to his blog.

Mr. Jarvis characterizes the blogging way of life as a routine rather
than an obsession. "It's a habit," he said. "What you're really doing is
telling people about something that they might find interesting.

When that becomes part of your life, when you start thinking in blog, it becomes part of you."

35   The constant search for bloggable moments is what led Gregor J. 35 Rothfuss, a programmer in Zurich, to blog to the point of near-despair. Bored by his job, Mr. Rothfuss, 27, started a blog that focused on technical topics.

"I was trying to record all thoughts and speculations I deemed interesting," he said. "Sort of creating a digital alter ego. The obsession came from trying to capture as much as possible of the good stuff in my head in as high fidelity as possible."

For months, Mr. Rothfuss said, he blogged at work, at home, late into the night, day in and day out until it all became a blur—all the while knowing, he added, "that no one was necessarily reading it, except for myself."

When traffic to the blog, greg.abstract.ch started to rise, he began devoting half a day every day and much of the weekend to it. Mr. Rothfuss said he has few memories of that period in his life aside from the compulsive blogging.

He was saved from the rut of his online chronicle when he traveled to Asia. The blog became more of a travelogue. Then Mr. Rothfuss switched jobs, finding one he enjoyed, and his blogging grew more moderate.

40   He still has the blog, but posts to it just twice a week, he said, "as 40 opposed to twice an hour." He feels healthier now. "It's part of what I do now, it's not what I do," he said.

Suffering from a similar form of "blog fatigue," Bill Barol, a free-lance writer in Santa Monica, Calif., simply stopped altogether after four years of nearly constant blogging.

"It was starting to feel like work, and it was never supposed to be a job," Mr. Barol said. "It was supposed to be an anti-job."

Even with some 200 visitors to his blog each day, he has not posted to his blog since returning from a month of travel.

Still, Mr. Barol said, he does not rule out a return to blogging someday.

45   "There is this seductive thing that happens, this kind of snowball- 45 rolling-down-a-hill thing, where the sheer momentum of several years' posting becomes very keenly felt," he said. "And the absence of posting feels like—I don't know, laziness or something."

I Think, Therefore IM

Jennifer Lee

*Jennifer Lee (1976–) was born in New York City. She grad-
uated from Harvard University in 1999 with a degree in
mathematics and economics. While at Harvard she spent a
year at Beijing University on a fellowship studying international relations. Lee has received a scholarship from the
Asian American Journalism Association and has interned at*
The Boston Globe, The New York Times, Newsday, The
Wall Street Journal, *and* The Washington Post. *She joined
the staff of* The New York Times *in 2001 as a technology
reporter and began writing for the Metro section the next
year. The following selection on instant-messaging language
originally appeared in the* Times *in September 2002.*

1   Each September Jacqueline Harding prepares a classroom presen-   1
tation on the common writing mistakes she sees in her students'
work.

Ms. Harding, an eighth-grade English teacher at Viking Middle
School in Guernee, Ill., scribbles the words that have plagued generations of school children across her whiteboard:

There. Their. They're.
Your. You're.
To. Too. Two.
Its. It's.

This September, she has added a new list: u, r, ur, b4, wuz, cuz, 2.

When she asked her students how many of them used shortcuts
like them in their writing, Ms. Harding said, she was not surprised
when most of them raised their hands. This, after all, is their online

lingua franca: English adapted for the spitfire conversational style of Internet instant messaging.

Ms. Harding, who has seen such shortcuts creep into student papers over the last two years, said she gave her students a warning: "If I see this in your assignments, I will take points off."

5   "Kids should know the difference," said Ms. Harding, who   5 decided to address this issue head-on this year. "They should know where to draw the line between formal writing and conversational writing."

As more and more teenagers socialize online, middle school and high school teachers like Ms. Harding are increasingly seeing a breezy form of Internet English jump from e-mail into schoolwork. To their dismay, teachers say that papers are being written with shortened words, improper capitalization and punctuation, and characters like &, $ and @.

Teachers have deducted points, drawn red circles and tsk-tsked at their classes. Yet the errant forms continue. "It stops being funny after you repeat yourself a couple of times," Ms. Harding said.

But teenagers, whose social life can rely as much these days on text communication as the spoken word, say that they use instant-messaging shorthand without thinking about it. They write to one another as much as they write in school, or more.

"You are so used to abbreviating things, you just start doing it unconsciously on schoolwork and reports and other things," said Eve Brecker, 15, a student at Montclair High School in New Jersey.

10   Ms. Brecker once handed in a midterm exam riddled with instant-   10 messaging shorthand. "I had an hour to write an essay on *Romeo and Juliet*," she said. "I just wanted to finish before my time was up. I was writing fast and carelessly. I spelled 'you' 'u.' " She got a C.

Even terms that cannot be expressed verbally are making their way into papers. Melanie Weaver was stunned by some of the term papers she received from a 10th-grade class she recently taught as part of an internship. "They would be trying to make a point in a paper, they would put a smiley face in the end," said Ms. Weaver, who teaches at Alvernia College in Reading, PA. "If they were presenting an argument and they needed to present an opposite view, they would put a frown."

As Trisha Fogarty, a sixth-grade teacher at Houlton Southside School in Houlton, Maine, puts it, today's students are "Generation Text."

Almost 60 percent of the online population under age 17 uses instant messaging, according to Nielsen/NetRatings. In addition to cellphone text messaging, Weblogs and e-mail, it has become a popular means of flirting, setting up dates, asking for help with homework and keeping in contact with distant friends. The abbreviations are a natural outgrowth of this rapid-fire style of communication.

"They have a social life that centers around typed communication," said Judith S. Donath, a professor at the Massachusetts Institute of Technology's Media Lab who has studied electronic communication. "They have a writing style that has been nurtured in a teenage social milieu."

15   Some teachers see the creeping abbreviations as part of a continuing assault of technology on formal written English. Others take it more lightly, saying that it is just part of the larger arc of language evolution.   15

"To them it's not wrong," said Ms. Harding, who is 28. "It's acceptable because it's in their culture. It's hard enough to teach them the art of formal writing. Now we've got to overcome this new instant-messaging language."

Ms. Harding noted that in some cases the shorthand isn't even shorter. "I understand 'cuz,' but what's with the 'wuz'? It's the same amount of letters as 'was,' so what's the point?" she said.

Deborah Bova, who teaches eighth-grade English at Raymond Park Middle School in Indianapolis, thought her eyesight was failing several years ago when she saw the sentence "B4 we perform, ppl have 2 practice" on a student assignment.

"I thought, 'My God, what is this?' " Ms. Bova said. "Have they lost their minds?"

20   The student was summoned to the board to translate the sentence into standard English: "Before we perform, people have to practice." She realized that the students thought she was out of touch. "It was like 'Get with it, Bova,' " she said. Ms. Bova had a student type up a reference list of translations for common instant-messaging expressions. She posted a copy on the bulletin board by her desk and took another one home to use while grading.   20

Students are sometimes unrepentant.

"They were astonished when I began to point these things out to them," said Henry Assetto, a social studies teacher at Twin Valley High School in Elverson, Pa. "Because I am a history teacher, they did not think a history teacher would be checking up on their grammar or their spelling," said Mr. Assetto, who has been teaching for 34 years.

But Montana Hodgen, 16, another Montclair student, said she was so accustomed to instant-messaging abbreviations that she often read right past them. She proofread a paper last year only to get it returned with the messaging abbreviations circled in red.

"I was so used to reading what my friends wrote to me on Instant Messenger that I didn't even realize that there was something wrong," she said. She said her ability to separate formal and informal English declined the more she used instant messages. "Three years ago, if I had seen that, I would have been 'What is that?' "

25   The spelling checker doesn't always help either, students say. For   25
one, Microsoft Word's squiggly red spell-check lines don't appear beneath single letters and numbers such as u, r, c, 2 and 4. Nor do they catch words which have numbers in them such as "l8r" and "b4" by default.

Teenagers have essentially developed an unconscious "accent" in their typing, Professor Donath said. "They have gotten facile at typing and they are not paying attention."

Teenagers have long pushed the boundaries of spoken language, introducing words that then become passe with adult adoption. Now teenagers are taking charge and pushing the boundaries of written language. For them, expressions like "oic" (oh I see), "nm" (not much), "jk" (just kidding) and "lol" (laughing out loud), "brb" (be right back), "ttyl" (talk to you later) are as standard as conventional English.

"There is no official English language," said Jesse Sheidlower, the North American editor of the *Oxford English Dictionary.* "Language is spread not because anyone dictates any one thing to happen. The decisions are made by the language and the people who use the language."

Some teachers find the new writing style alarming. "First of all, it's very rude, and it's very careless," said Lois Moran, a middle school English teacher at St. Nicholas School in Jersey City.

30   "They should be careful to write properly and not to put these little   30
codes in that they are in such a habit of writing to each other," said Ms. Moran, who has lectured her eighth-grade class on such mistakes.

Others say that the instant-messaging style might simply be a fad, something that students will grow out of. Or they see it as an opportunity to teach students about the evolution of language.

"I turn it into a very positive teachable moment for kids in the class," said Erika V. Karres, an assistant professor at the University of North Carolina at Chapel Hill who trains student teachers. She shows students how English has evolved since Shakespeare's time. "Imagine Langston Hughes's writing in quick texting instead of 'Langston writing,' " she said. "It makes teaching and learning so exciting."

Other teachers encourage students to use messaging shorthand to spark their thinking processes. "When my children are writing first drafts, I don't care how they spell anything, as long as they are writing," said Ms. Fogarty, the sixth-grade teacher from Houlton, Maine. "If this lingo gets their thoughts and ideas onto paper quicker, the more power to them." But during editing and revising, she expects her students to switch to standard English.

Ms. Bova shares the view that instant-messaging language can help free up their creativity. With the help of students, she does not even need the cheat sheet to read the shorthand anymore.

35 "I think it's a plus," she said. "And I would say that with a + sign." 35

Finding One's Own Space in Cyberspace

Amy Bruckman

Amy Bruckman teaches in the College of Computing at Georgia Tech, having completed a Ph.D. in the Epistemology and Learning Group at the MIT Media Lab. While still a graduate student, Bruckman founded two virtual communities, MediaMOO (for media researchers) and MOOSE Crossing (for children), the latter the subject of her dissertation. In the article from Technology Review *reprinted here, she describes the new rules emerging as people form societies that exist only when people are online together.*

1   The week the last Internet porn scandal broke, my phone didn't stop ringing: "Are women comfortable on the Net?" "Should women use gender neutral names on the Net?" "Are women harassed on the Net?" Reporters called from all over the country with basically the same question. I told them all: your question is ill-formed. "The Net" is not one thing. It's like asking: "Are women comfortable in bars?" That's a silly question. Which woman? Which bar?

   The summer I was 18, I was the computer counselor at a summer camp. After the campers were asleep, the counselors were allowed out, and would go bar hopping. First everyone would go to Maria's, an Italian restaurant with red-and-white-checkered table cloths. Maria welcomed everyone from behind the bar, greeting regular customers by name. She always brought us free garlic bread. Next we'd go to the Sandpiper, a disco with good dance music. The Sandpiper seemed excitingly adult—it was a little scary at first, but then I loved it. Next, we went to the Sportsman, a leather motorcycle bar that I found

From *Technology Review* 99, No. 1 (January 1996). Copyright © 1996 by Alumni Association of The Massachusetts Institute of Technology.

absolutely terrifying. Huge, bearded men bulging out of their leather vests and pants leered at me. I hid in the corner and tried not to make eye contact with anyone, hoping my friends would get tired soon and give me a ride back to camp.

Each of these bars was a community, and some were more comfortable for me than others. The Net is made up of hundreds of thousands of separate communities, each with its own special character. Not only is the Net a diverse place, but "women" are diverse as well—there were leather-clad women who loved the Sportsman, and plenty of women revel in the fiery rhetoric of Usenet's alt.flame. When people complain about being harassed on the Net, they've usually stumbled into the wrong online community. The question is not whether "women" are comfortable on "the Net," but rather, what types of communities are possible? How can we create a range of communities so that everyone—men and women—can find a place that is comfortable for them?

If you're looking for a restaurant or bar, you can often tell without even going in: Is the sign flashing neon or engraved wood? Are there lots of cars parked out front? What sort of cars? (You can see all the Harleys in front of the Sportsman from a block away.) Look in the window: How are people dressed? We are accustomed to diversity in restaurants. People know that not all restaurants will please them, and employ a variety of techniques to choose the right one.

5   It's a lot harder to find a good virtual community than it is to find   5
a good bar. The visual cues that let you spot the difference between Maria's and the Sportsman from across the street are largely missing. Instead, you have to "lurk"—enter the community and quietly explore for a while, getting the feel of whether it's the kind of place you're looking for. Although published guides exist, they're not always very useful—most contain encyclopedic lists with little commentary or critical evaluation, and by the time they're published they're already out of date. Magazines like *NetGuide* and *Wired* are more current and more selective, and therefore more useful, but their editorial bias may not fit with your personal tastes.

Commonly available network-searching tools are also useful. The World Wide Web is filled with searching programs, indexes, and even indexes of indexes ("meta-indexes"). Although browsing with these tools can be a pleasant diversion, it is not very efficient, and searches for particular pieces of information often end in frustration. If you keep an open mind, however, you may come across something good.

Shaping an Online Society

But what happens if, after exploring and asking around, you still can't find an online environment that suits you? Don't give up: start your own! This doesn't have to be a difficult task. Anyone can create a new newsgroup in Usenet's "alt" hierarchy or open a new chat room on America Online. Users of Unix systems can easily start a mailing list. If you have a good idea but not enough technical skill or the right type of Net access, there are people around eager to help. The more interesting question is: How do you help a community to become what you hope for? Here, I can offer some hard-won advice.

In my research at the MIT Media Lab (working with Professor Mitchel Resnick), I design virtual communities. In October of 1992, I founded a professional community for media researchers on the Internet called MediaMOO. Over the past three years, as MediaMOO has grown to 1,000 members from 33 countries, I have grappled with many of the issues that face anyone attempting to establish a virtual community. MediaMOO is a "multi-user dungeon" or MUD—A virtual world on the Internet with rooms, objects, and people from all around the world. Messages typed in by a user instantly appear on the screens of all other users who are currently in the same virtual "room." This real-time interaction distinguishes MUDs from Usenet newsgroups, where users can browse through messages created many hours or days before. The MUD's virtual world is built in text descriptions. MOO stands for MUD object-oriented, a kind of MUD software (created by Pavel Curtis of the Xerox Palo Alto Research Center and Stephen White, now at InContext Systems) that allows each user to write programs to define spaces and objects.

The first MUDS, developed in the late 1970s, were multiplayer fantasy games of the dungeons-and-dragons variety. In 1989, a graduate student at Carnegie Mellon University named James Aspnes decided to see what would happen if you took away the monsters and the magic swords but instead let people extend the virtual world. People's main activity went from trying to conquer the virtual world to trying to build it, collaboratively.

10 Most MUDs are populated by undergraduates who should be 10 doing their homework. I thought it would be interesting instead to bring together a group of people with a shared intellectual interest: the study of media. Ideally, MediaMOO should be like an endless

reception for a conference on media studies. But given the origin of MUDs as violent games, giving one an intellectual and professional atmosphere was a tall order. How do you guide the evolution of who uses the space and what they do there?

A founder/designer can't control what the community ultimately becomes—much of that is up to the users—but can help shape it. The personality of the community's founder can have a great influence on what sort of place it becomes. Part of what made Maria's so comfortable for me was Maria herself. She radiated a warmth that made me feel at home.

Similarly, one of the most female-friendly electronic communities I've visited is New York City's ECHO (East Coast Hang Out) bulletin board, run by Stacy Horn. Smart, stylish, and deliberately outrageous, Horn is role model and patron saint for the ECHO-ites. Her outspoken but sensitive personality infuses the community, and sends a message to women that it's all right to speak up. She added a conference to ECHO called "WIT" (women in telecommunications), which one user describes as "a warm, supportive, women-only, private conference where women's thoughts, experiences, wisdom, joys, and despairs are shared." But Horn also added a conference called "BITCH," which the ECHO-ite calls "WIT in black leather jackets. All-women, riotous and raunchy."

Horn's high-energy, very New York brand of intelligence establishes the kind of place ECHO is and influences how everyone there behaves. When ECHO was first established, Horn and a small group of her close friends were the most active people on the system. "That set the emotional tone, the traditional style of posting, the unwritten rules about what it's OK to say," says Marisa Bowe, an ECHO administrator for many years. "Even though Stacy is too busy these days to post very much, the tone established in the early days continues," says Bowe, who is now editor of an online magazine called *Word*.

Beyond the sheer force of a founder's personality, a community establishes a particular character with a variety of choices on how to operate. One example is to set a policy on whether to allow participants to remain anonymous. Initially, I decided that members of MediaMOO should be allowed to choose: they could identify themselves with their real names and e-mail addresses, or remain anonymous. Others questioned whether there was a role for anonymity in a professional community.

15   As time went on, I realized they were right. People on Media- 15
MOO are supposed to be networking, hoping someone will look up
who they really are and where they work. Members who are not willing to share their personal and professional identities are less likely to
engage in serious discussion about their work, and consequently about
media in general. Furthermore, comments from an anonymous entity
are less valuable because they are unsituated—"I believe X" is less
meaningful to a listener than "I am a librarian with eight years of experience who lives in a small town in Georgia, and I believe X." In
theory, anonymous participants could describe their professional experiences and place their comments in that context; in practice it
tends not to happen that way. After six months, I proposed that we
change the policy to require that all new members be identified. Despite the protests of a few vocal opponents, most people thought that
this was a good idea, and the change was made.

Each community needs to have its own policy on anonymity.
There's room for diversity here too: some communities can be all-
anonymous, some all-identified, and some can leave that decision up
to each individual. An aside: right now on the Net no one is either really anonymous or really identified. It is easy to fake an identity; it is
also possible to use either technical or legal tools to peer behind someone else's veil of anonymity. This ambiguous state of affairs is not necessarily unfortunate: it's nice to know that a fake identity that provides
a modicum of privacy is easy to construct, but that in extreme cases
such people can be tracked down.

Finding Birds of a Feather

Another important design decision is admissions policy. Most places
on the Net have a strong pluralistic flavor, and the idea that some people might be excluded from a community ruffles a lot of feathers. But
exclusivity is a fact of life. MIT wouldn't be MIT if everyone who
wanted to come was admitted. Imagine if companies had to give jobs
to everyone who applied! Virtual communities, social clubs, universi-
ties, and corporations are all groups of people brought together for a
purpose. Achieving that purpose often requires that there be some way
to determine who can join the community

A key decision I made for MediaMOO was to allow entry only to
people doing some sort of "media research." I try to be loose on the

definition of "media"—writing teachers, computer network adminis-trators, and librarians are all working with forms of media—but strict on the definition of "research." At first, this policy made me uncom-fortable. I would nervously tell people, "It's mostly a self-selection process. We hardly reject anyone at all!" Over time, I've become more comfortable with this restriction, and have enforced the requirements more stringently. I now believe my initial unease was naive.

Even if an online community decides to admit all comers, it does not have to let all contributors say anything they want. The existence of a moderator to filter postings often makes for more focused and civil discussion. Consider Usenet's two principal newsgroups dealing with feminism—alt.feminism and soc.feminism. In alt.feminism, anyone can post whatever they want. Messages in this group are filled with the angry words of angry people; more insults than ideas are ex-changed. (Titles of messages found there on a randomly selected day included "Women & the workplace (it doesn't work)" and "What is a feminazi?") The topic may nominally be feminism, but the discussion itself is not feminist in nature.

20 The huge volume of postings (more than 200 per day, on average) 20 shows that many people enjoy writing such tirades. But if I wanted to discuss some aspect of feminism, alt.feminism would be the last place I'd go. Its sister group, soc.feminism, is moderated—volunteers read messages submitted to the group and post only those that pass muster. Moderators adhere to soc.feminism's lengthy charter, which explains the criteria for acceptable postings—forbidding ad hominem attacks, for instance.

Moderation of a newsgroup, like restricting admission to a MUD, grants certain individuals within a community power over others. If only one group could exist, I'd have to choose the uncensored alt.fem-inism to the moderated soc.feminism. Similarly, if MediaMOO were the only virtual community or MIT the only university, I'd argue that they should be open to all. However, there are thousands of universi-ties and the Net contains hundreds of thousands of virtual communi-ties, with varying criteria for acceptable conduct. That leaves room for diversity: some communities can be moderated, others unmoderated. Some can be open to all, some can restrict admissions.

The way a community is publicized—or not publicized—also in-fluences its character. Selective advertising can help a community achieve a desired ambiance. In starting up MediaMOO, for example, we posted the original announcement to mailing lists for different aspects of media studies—not to the general-purpose groups for discussing MUDs on Usenet. MediaMOO is now rarely if ever deliberately advertised. The group has opted not to be listed in the public, published list of MUDs on the Internet. Members are asked to mention MediaMOO to other groups only if the majority of members of that group would probably be eligible to join MediaMOO.

New members are attracted by word of mouth among media researchers. To bring in an influx of new members, MediaMOO typically "advertises" by organizing an online discussion or symposium on some aspect of media studies. Announcing a discussion group on such topics as the techniques for studying behavior in a virtual community, or strategies for using computers to teach writing, attracts the right sort of people to the community and sets a tone for the kinds of discussion that take place there. That's much more effective than a more general announcement of MediaMOO and its purpose.

In an ideal world, virtual communities would acquire new members entirely by self-selection: people would enter an electronic neighborhood only if it focused on something they cared about. In most cases, this process works well. For example, one Usenet group that I sometimes read—sci.aquaria—attracts people who are really interested in discussing tropical fishkeeping. But self-selection is not always sufficient. For example, the challenge of making MediaMOO's culture different from prevailing MUD culture made self-selection inadequate. Lots of undergraduates with no particular focus to their interests want to join MediaMOO. To preserve MediaMOO's character as a place for serious scholarly discussions, I usually reject these applications. Besides, almost all of the hundreds of other MUDs out there place no restrictions on who can join. MediaMOO is one of the few that is different.

25 Emotionally and politically charged subject matter, such as feminism, makes it essential for members of a community to have a shared understanding of the community's purpose. People who are interested in freshwater and saltwater tanks can coexist peacefully in parallel conversations on sci.aquaria. However, on alt.feminism, people who want to explore the implications of feminist theory, and those who want to question its basic premises, don't get along quite so well. Self-selection alone is not adequate for bringing together a group to discuss a hot topic. People with radically differing views may wander in innocently, 25

or barge in deliberately—disrupting the conversation through igno-rance or malice.

Such gate crashing tends to occur more frequently as the com-munity grows in size. For example, some participants in the Usenet group alt.tasteless decided to post a series of grotesque messages to the thriving group rec.pets.cats, including recipes for how to cook cat. A small, low-profile group may be randomly harassed, but that's less likely to happen.

In the offline world, membership in many social organizations is open only to those who are willing and able to pay the dues. While it may rankle an American pluralistic sensibility, the use of wealth as a social filter has the advantages of simplicity and objectivity: no one's personal judgment plays a role in deciding who is to be admitted. And imposing a small financial hurdle to online participation may do more good than harm. Token fees discourage the random and pointless postings that dilute the value of many newsgroups. One of the first community networks, Community Memory in Berkeley, Calif., found that charging a mere 25 cents to post a message significantly raised the level of discourse, eliminating many trivial or rude messages.

Still, as the fee for participation rises above a token level, this method has obvious moral problems for a society committed to equal opportunity. In instituting any kind of exclusionary policy, the founder of a virtual community should first test the key assumption that alternative, nonexclusionary communities really do exist. If they do not, then less restrictive admissions policies may be warranted.

Building on Diversity

Anonymity policy, admissions requirements, and advertising strategy all contribute to a virtual community's character. Without such meth-ods of distinguishing one online hangout from another, all would tend to sink to the least common denominator of discourse—the equiva-lent of every restaurant in a town degenerating into a dive. We need better techniques to help members of communities develop shared ex-pectations about the nature of the community, and to communicate those expectations to potential new members. This will make it easier for people to find their own right communities.

30 Just as the surest way to find a good restaurant is to exchange tips 30 with friends, word of mouth is usually the best way to find out about

virtual communities that might suit your tastes and interests. The best published guides for restaurants compile comments and ratings from a large group of patrons, rather than relying on the judgment of any one expert. Approaches like this are being explored on the Net. Yezdi Lashkari, cofounder of Agents Inc., designed a system called "Webhound" that recommends items of interest on the World Wide Web. To use Webhound, you enter into the system a list of web sites you like. It matches you with people of similar interests, and then recommends other sites that they like. Not only do these ratings come from an aggregate of many opinions, but they also are matched to your personal preferences.

Webhound recommends just World Wide Web pages, but the same basic approach could help people find a variety of communities, products, and services that are likely to match their tastes. For example, Webhound grew out of the Helpful Online Music Recommendation Service (HOMR), which recommends musical artists. A subscriber to this service—recently renamed Firefly—first rates a few dozen musical groups on a scale from "the best" to "pass the earplugs"; Firefly searches its database for people who have similar tastes, and uses their list of favorites to recommend other artists that might appeal to you. The same technique could recommend Usenet newsgroups, mailing lists, or other information sources. Tell it that you like to read the Usenet group "rec.arts. startrek.info," and it might recommend "alt.tv.babylon-5"—people who like one tend to like the other. While no such tool yet exists for Usenet, the concept would be straightforward to implement.

Written statements of purpose and codes of conduct can help communities stay focused and appropriate. MediaMOO's stated purpose, for example, helps set its character as an arena for scholarly discussion. But explicit rules and mission statements can go only so far. Elegant restaurants don't put signs on the door saying "no feet on tables" and fast food restaurants don't post signs saying "feet on tables allowed." Subtle cues within the environment indicate how one is expected to behave. Similarly, we should design regions in cyberspace so that people implicitly sense what is expected and what is appropriate. In this respect, designers of virtual communities can learn a great deal from architects.

Vitruvius, a Roman architect from the first century B.C., established the basic principle of architecture as commodity (appropriate function), firmness (structural stability), and delight. These principles translate into the online world, as William Mitchell, dean of MIT's School of Architecture and Planning, points out in his book *City of Bits: Space, Place, and the Infobahn.*

Architects of the twenty-first century will still shape, arrange and connect spaces (both real and virtual) to satisfy human needs. They will still care about the qualities of visual and ambient environments. They will still seek commodity, firmness, and delight. But commodity will be as much a matter of software functions and interface design as it is of floor plans and construction materials. Firmness will entail not only the physical integrity of structural systems, but also the logical integrity of computer systems. And delight? Delight will have unimagined new dimensions.

35   Marcos Novak of the University of Texas at Austin is exploring 35
some of those "unimagined dimensions" with his notion of a "liquid architecture" for cyberspace, free from the constraints of physical space and building materials. But work of this kind on the merging of architecture and software design is regrettably rare; if virtual communities are buildings, then right now we are living in the equivalent of thatched huts. If the structure keeps out the rain—that is, if the software works at all—people are happy.

More important than the use of any of these particular techniques, however, is applying an architect's design sensibility to this new medium. Many of the traditional tools and techniques of architects, such as lighting and texture, will translate into the design of virtual environments. Depending on choice of background color and texture, type styles, and special fade-in effects, for instance, a Web page can feel playful or gloomy, futuristic or old-fashioned, serious or fun, grown-up or child-centered. The language of the welcoming screen, too, conveys a sense of the community's purpose and character. An opening screen thick with the jargon of specialists in, say, genetic engineering, might alert dilettantes that the community is for serious biologists.

As the Net expands, its ranks will fill with novices—some of whom, inevitably, will wander into less desirable parts of cybertown. It is important for such explorers to appreciate the Net's diversity—to realize, for example, that the newsgroup alt.feminism does not constitute the Internet's sole contribution to feminist debate. Alternatives exist.

I'm glad there are places on the Net where I'm not comfortable. The world would be a boring place if it invariably suited any one person's taste. The great promise of the Net is diversity. That's something we need to cultivate and cherish. Unfortunately, there aren't yet enough good alternatives—too much of the Net is like the Sportsman and too little of it is like Maria's. Furthermore, not enough people are aware that communities can have such different characters.

People who accidentally find themselves in the Sportsman, alt.feminism, or alt.flame, and don't find the black leather or fiery insults to their liking, should neither complain about it nor waste their time there—they should search for a more suitable community. If you've stumbled into the wrong town, get back on the bus. But if you've been a long-time resident and find the community changing for the worse—that's different. Don't shy away from taking political action within that community to protect your investment of time: speak up, propose solutions, and build a coalition of others who feel the same way you do.

40   With the explosion of interest in networking, people are moving 40 from being recipients of information to creators, from passive subscribers to active participants and leaders. Newcomers to the Net who are put off by harassment, pornography, and just plain bad manners should stop whining about the places they find unsuitable and turn their energies in a more constructive direction: help make people aware of the variety of alternatives that exist, and work to build communities that suit their interests and values.

Remixing/Technological Literacies

Culture in the Arab World by Shereen El Feki
Laws that Choke Creativity by Larry Lesig
Chris Jordan Pictures Some Shocking Stats by Chris
Jordan

Revising Literacies

Revising Literacies

You probably have at least a little bit of a different idea about literacy than you had when you wrote your first paper. In this section, we present some essays in which writers talk with us about how their views of some notions of literacy have changed and/or how literacy has helped them make a change. Remember to think about invention, arrangement, revision and delivery as you read. Although chances are you have discussed style throughout the semester, at this point think about how the style the writer uses helps or hinders the text's revisionary purpose.

As you prepare to compose your final project, think about what significant changes have occurred in your ideas about literacy, in your literacy practices, and in your understanding of how literacy will affect you life in the future. How might what you have learned become part of one of the larger conversations about literacy you have been introduced to this semester?

Writing Is my Passion

bell hooks

bell hooks (1952–), the pseudonym of Gloria Watkins, was born in Kentucky. She received a B.A. from Stanford University and a Ph.D. from the University of California, Santa Cruz. An advocate for African-American women in the feminist movement as well as a critic of the white male–dominated U.S. power structure, hooks has taught at Oberlin College and Yale University. Her books include Ain't I a Woman: Black Women and Feminism *(1981),* Feminist Theory: From Margin to Center *(1984),* Talking Back: Thinking Feminist, Thinking Black *(1989),* Yearning: Race, Gender, and Cultural Politics *(1990),* Breaking Bread: Insurgent Black Intellectual Life *(1992),* Black Looks: Race and Representation *(1992),* Outlaw Culture *(1994),* Teaching to Transgress: Education as the Practice of Freedom *(1994),* Reel to Real: Race, Sex, and Class at the Movies *(1996), and* Remembering Rapture *(1999). The following selection is a chapter from* Wounds of Passion: A Writing Life *(1997).*

1   Writing is my passion. Words are the way to know ecstasy. Without them life is barren. The poet insists *Language is a body of suffering and when you take up language you take up the suffering too.* All my life I have been suffering for words. Words have been the source of the pain and the way to heal.

Struck as a child for talking, for speaking out of turn, for being out of my place. Struck as a grown woman for not knowing when to shut up, for not being willing to sacrifice words for desire. Struck by writing a book that disrupts. There are many ways to be hit. Pain is the price we pay to speak the truth. *Language is a body of suffering and when you take up language you take up the suffering too.*

Nothing is as simple as it seems, so much is neither good nor bad, but always a blend of truths. In the household of my childhood, that place where I was held prisoner, there was no doubt in anyone's mind that I would write, that I would become a writer, magician of words, one who suffers well. *She works hard in the name of love. She who is able to sacrifice.*

Nothing is as simple as it seems. No one in the house of my childhood doubts my power to create. I learn doubt when I leave home I learn to doubt my intelligence, my creativity in the integrated world—at college and in the arms of talented men. They try and teach me to fear a woman's word, to doubt whether her words can ever be as good, as perfect as any man's sound. No wonder then there is something in me that clings to childhood—to the girl who loved Emily Dickinson, writer, thinker, dreamer of worlds. In the shadow of her presence, I am without doubt. I know I can become a writer.

5 *She stayed with him much longer than she should have. Her staying was never a way to cling to love. She feared losing the discipline to write. She entered a committed relationship so soon, so young devote herself to writing. So much in the world distracted her from words. So much made life seem crazy. At times she dreamed of returning home. Despite all the madness of home, she had always found a place to read, contemplate life, and write there.*

She is right. Nothing is as simple as it seems. You would think all those fancy colleges she went to so far away from home would have made it easy to write. Baba used to asked her How can you live so far away from your people. At home she doubted her capacity to love, to be intimate, to make friends even. Introverted and awkward she doubted so much about herself but never her ability to imagine, to write.

No one really says how it will be. When we try to leave behind all the limits of race and gender and class, to transcend them, to get to the heart of the matter. No one really says how painful it will be—that just when you think you are moving forward in life some new thing, another barrier surfaces that just stops you in your tracks. For all that goes wrong in my life with Mack, I have had shelter here, a sanctuary for that part of me that was destined to write, to make a life in words.

Language is a body of suffering and when you take up language you take up the suffering too.

Nobody ever talked to us about how we would become these new women and men transformed by feminist movement. All the cultural revolutions created by black liberation and sexual liberation and women's liberation, and yet there is still no map—nothing that will guide us safely to mutual love and respect. We lose our way. One thing is certain—we can never turn back.

After all our feminist victory, there is still a grave silence about the issue of whether women can be in love relationships with men and truly develop as writers. I believe my relationship with Mack strengthens me as a thinker and a writer. I used to say that we were better at giving each other the space to be independent than we were at being together. I grew stronger as a writer at all times, even during times when we were in crisis. Writing was my refuge and my rescue.

10 *She believed for so long that if she left their relationship she might cease to* 10 *write. After all she became a disciplined published writer there in the shadows of their love. To depart from that love might mean to depart from writing. She could imagine living without him. She could not imagine living without words. And so she remained.*

They all wanted to know *Why did you stay with him so long.* I am weary explaining. Doesn't everyone realize that nothing is as simple as it seems. Our relationship falling apart is no one's fault. Everybody wants somebody to blame. I wanted to make sense of the pain. The ways I was hurt in this relationship and the ways I hurt were only one fragment of a larger piece. When I left home, I thought I was leaving hurt behind. I did not even imagine that there were ways to be hurt in the world outside home. When you are confined to a small segregated area across the tracks, away from so much going on in the larger world, innocence is still possible. Measured against the pain in the world, home seemed a safe haven, both the home I left and the home I had made with Mack.

To explain things she says: Every terrorist regime in the world uses isolation to break the human spirit. It is not difficult for her to see that women writers, especially black women writers, are isolated. She can count the ones whose work is recognized. She can see for herself how many die alone, unloved, their work forgotten. She can see for herself how many remain invisible. She can see how many go mad.

Haunted by the fear of madness, I am deeply convinced that the world is not a safe place for me. I remain reluctant to move, to change, to go anywhere. I need company to move outside the home. That was the way it was growing up. A girl was never left alone. When I came to college I realized I had never been alone not even for a day. Whenever we left the house as girls we were escorted. In private I love to be alone. In public I prefer company.

They were always so together the two of them. They did everything together. No wonder then it was surprising that they could not work together in the same room. In private they were alone, they were silent. In private they were devoted to work.

15 Women sacrifice for words. They suffer and they die. The poet Audre 15 Lorde visits our house. She sits and flirts on our Victorian deep red couch. She has just autographed a copy of my favorite poem "Litany for Survival." Her words say everything there is to say about the perils the exploited and the oppressed face coming to voice. She goes straight to the heart of the matter: *When we are loved we are afraid love will vanish / when we are alone we are afraid love will never return / and when we speak we are afraid our words will not be heard not welcome / but when we are silent we are still afraid.*

Professions for Women

Virginia Woolf

Virginia Woolf (1882–1941) was born in London. She was educated at home by her father, a well-known writer and scholar. As a young woman, she became a member of the Bloomsbury Group of writers and artists in London. In 1912, she wed author and publisher Leonard Woolf, another member of the Bloomsbury Group; together they set up Hogarth Press, which published much of her work. Woolf, who suffered from depression throughout her life, committed suicide in her late fifties. Woolf's publications include the novels Mrs. Dalloway *(1925),* To the Lighthouse *(1927), and* The Waves *(1931) and the essay collections* A Room of One's Own *(1920) and* The Death of the Moth and Other Essays *(1948). Known for her impressionistic, stream-of-consciousness style, Woolf is a dominant force in English literature. This essay, written as a speech that Woolf presented to the Women's Service League in 1931, presents Woolf's view of employment hurdles facing women.*

1   When your secretary invited me to come here, she told me that your Society is concerned with the employment of women and she suggested that I might tell you something about my own professional experiences. It is true I am a woman; it is true I am employed; but what professional experiences have I had? It is difficult to say. My profession is literature; and in that profession there are fewer experiences for women than in any other, with the exception of the stage—fewer, I mean, that are peculiar to women. For the road was cut many years ago—by Fanny Burney, by Aphra Behn,

by Harriet Martineau, by Jane Austen, by George Eliot—many famous women, and many more unknown and forgotten, have been before me, making the path smooth, and regulating my steps. Thus, when I came to write, there were very few material obstacles in my way. Writing was a reputable and harmless occupation. The family peace was not broken by the scratching of a pen. No demand was made upon the family purse. For ten and sixpence one can buy paper enough to write all the plays of Shakespeare—if one has a mind that way. Pianos and models, Paris, Vienna and Berlin, masters and mistresses, are not needed by a writer. The cheapness of writing paper is, of course, the reason why women have succeeded as writers before they have succeeded in the other professions.

But to tell you my story—it is a simple one. You have only got to figure to yourselves a girl in a bedroom with a pen in her hand. She had only to move that pen from left to right—from ten o'clock to one. Then it occurred to her to do what is simple and cheap enough after all—to slip a few of those pages into an envelope, fix a penny stamp in the corner, and drop the envelope into the red box at the corner. It was thus that I became a journalist; and my effort was rewarded on the first day of the following month—a very glorious day it was for me—by a letter from an editor containing a cheque for one pound ten shillings and sixpence. But to show you how little I deserve to be called a professional woman, how little I know of the struggles and difficulties of such lives, I have to admit that instead of spending that sum upon bread and butter, rent, shoes and stockings, or butcher's bills, I went out and bought a cat—a beautiful cat, a Persian cat, which very soon involved me in bitter disputes with my neighbors.

What could be easier than to write articles and to buy Persian cats with the profits? But wait a moment. Articles have to be about something. Mine, I seem to remember, was about a novel by a famous man. And while I was writing this review, I discovered that if I were going to review books I should need to do battle with a certain phantom. And the phantom was a woman, and when I came to know her better I called her after the heroine of a famous poem, "The Angel in the House." It was she who used to come between me and my paper when I was writing reviews. It was she who bothered me and wasted my time and so tormented me that at last I killed her. You who come of a younger and happier generation may not have heard of her—you may not know what I mean by the Angel in the House. I will describe her as shortly as I can. She was intensely sympathetic. She was immensely charming. She was utterly unselfish. She excelled in the difficult arts of family life. She sacrificed herself daily. If there was chicken, she took the leg; if there was a draught she sat in it—in short she was so constituted that she never had a mind or a wish of her own, but preferred to sympathize always with the minds and wishes of others. Above all—I need not say it—she was pure. Her purity was supposed to be her chief beauty—her blushes, her great grace. In those days—the last of Queen Victoria—every house had its Angel. And when I came to write I encountered her with the very first words. The shadow of her wings fell on my page; I heard the rustling of her skirts in the room. Directly, that is to say, I took my pen in hand to review that novel by a famous man, she slipped behind me and whispered: "My dear, you are a young woman. You are writing about a book that has been written by a man. Be sympathetic; be tender; flatter; deceive; use all the arts and wiles of our sex. Never let anybody guess that you have a mind of your own. Above all, be pure." And she made as if to guide my pen. I now record the one act for which I take some credit to myself, though the credit rightly belongs to some excellent ancestors of mine who left me a certain sum of money—shall we say five hundred pounds a year?—so that it was not necessary for me to depend solely on charm for my living. I turned upon her and caught her by the throat. I did my best to kill her. My excuse, if I were to be had up in a court of law, would be that I acted in self-defence. Had I not killed her she would have killed me. She would have plucked the heart out of my writing. For, as I found, directly I put pen to paper, you cannot review even a novel without having a mind of your own, without expressing what you think to be the truth about human relations, morality, sex. And all these questions, according to the Angel in the House, cannot be dealt with freely and openly by women; they must charm, they must conciliate, they must—to put it bluntly—tell lies if they are to succeed. Thus, whenever I felt the shadow of her wing or the radiance of her halo upon my page, I took up the inkpot and flung it at her. She died hard. Her fictitious nature was of great assistance to her. It is far harder to kill a phantom than a reality. She was always creeping back when I thought I had despatched her. Though I flatter myself that I killed her in the end, the struggle was severe; it took much time that had better have been spent upon learning Greek grammar; or in roaming the world in search of adventures. But it was a real experience; it was an experience that was bound to befall all women writers at that time. Killing the Angel in the House was part of the occupation of a woman writer.

But to continue my story. The Angel was dead; what then remained? You may say that what remained was a simple and common object—a young woman in a bedroom with an inkpot. In other words, now that she had rid herself of falsehood, that young woman had only to be herself. Ah, but what is "herself"? I mean, what is a woman? I assure you, I do not know. I do not believe that you know. I do not believe that anybody can know until she has expressed herself in all the arts and professions open to human skill. That indeed is one of the reasons why I have come here—out of respect for you, who are in process of showing us by your experiments what a woman is, who are in process of providing us, by your failures and successes, with that extremely important piece of information.

5 But to continue the story of my professional experiences. I made 5 one pound ten and six by my first review; and I bought a Persian cat with the proceeds. Then I grew ambitious. A Persian cat is all very well, I said; but a Persian cat is not enough. I must have a motor car. And it was thus that I became a novelist—for it is a very strange thing that people will give you a motor car if you will tell them a story. It is a still stranger thing that there is nothing so delightful in the world as telling stories. It is far pleasanter than writing reviews of famous novels. And yet, if I am to obey your secretary and tell you my professional experiences as a novelist, I must tell you about a very strange experience that befell me as a novelist. And to understand it you must try first to imagine a novelist's state of mind. I hope I am not giving away professional secrets if I say that a novelist's chief desire is to be as unconscious as possible. He has to induce in himself a state of perpetual lethargy. He wants life to proceed with the utmost quiet and regularity. He wants to see the same faces, to read the same books, to do the same things day after day, month after month, while he is writing, so that nothing may break the illusion in which he is living—so that nothing may disturb or disquiet the mysterious nosings about, feelings round, darts, dashes and sudden discoveries of that very shy and illusive spirit, the imagination. I suspect that this state is the same both for men and women. Be that as it may, I want you to imagine me writing a novel in a state of trance. I want you to figure to yourself a girl sitting with a pen in her hand, which for minutes, and indeed for hours, she never dips into the inkpot. The image that comes

to my mind when I think of this girl is the image of a fisherman lying sunk in dreams on the verge of a deep lake with a rod held out over the water. She was letting her imagination sweep unchecked round every rock and cranny of the world that lies submerged in the depths of our unconscious being. Now came the experience, the experience that I believe to be far commoner with women writers than with men. The line raced through the girl's fingers. Her imagination had rushed away. It had sought the pools, the depths, the dark places where the largest fish slumber. And then there was a smash. There was an explosion. There was foam and confusion. The imagination had dashed itself against something hard. The girl was roused from her dream. She was indeed in a state of the most acute and difficult distress. To speak without figure she had thought of something, something about the body, about the passions which it was unfitting for her as a woman to say. Men, her reason told her, would be shocked. The consciousness of what men will say of a woman who speaks the truth about her passions had roused her from her artist's state of unconsciousness. She could write no more. The trance was over. Her imagination could work no longer. This I believe to be a very common experience with women writers—they are impeded by the extreme conventionality of the other sex. For though men sensibly allow themselves great freedom in these respects, I doubt that they realize or can control the extreme severity with which they condemn such freedom in women.

These then were two very genuine experiences of my own. These were two of the adventures of my professional life. The first—killing the Angel in the House—I think I solved. She died. But the second, telling the truth about my own experiences as a body, I do not think I solved. I doubt that any woman has solved it yet. The obstacles against her are still immensely powerful—and yet they are very difficult to define. Outwardly, what is simpler than to write books? Outwardly, what obstacles are there for a woman rather than for a man? Inwardly, I think, the case is very different: she has still many ghosts to fight, many prejudices to overcome. Indeed it will be a long time still, I think, before a woman can sit down to write a book without finding a phantom to be slain, a rock to be dashed against. And if this is so in literature, the freest of all professions for women, how is it in the new professions which you are now for the first time entering?

Those are the questions that I should like, had I time, to ask you. And indeed, if I have laid stress upon these professional experiences of mine, it is because I believe that they are, though in different forms, yours also. Even when the path is nominally open—when there is nothing to prevent a woman from being a doctor, a lawyer, a civil servant—there are many phantoms and obstacles, as I believe, looming in her way. To discuss and define them is, I think, of great value and importance; for thus only can the labour be shared, the difficulties be solved. But besides this, it is necessary also to discuss the ends and the aims for which we are fighting, for which we are doing battle with these formidable obstacles. Those aims cannot be taken for granted; they must be perpetually questioned and examined. The whole position, as I see it—here in this hall surrounded by women practicing for the first time in history I know not how many different professions—is one of extraordinary interest and importance. You have won rooms of your own in the house hitherto exclusively owned by men. You are able, though not without great labor and effort, to pay the rent. You are earning your five hundred pounds a year. But this freedom is only a beginning; the room is your own, but it is still bare. It has to be furnished; it has to be decorated; it has to be shared. How are you going to furnish it, how are you going to decorate it? With whom are you going to share it, and upon what terms? These, I think, are questions of the utmost importance and interest. For the first time in history you are able to ask them; for the first time you are able to decide for yourselves what the answers should be. Willingly would I stay and discuss those questions and answers—but not tonight. My time is up; and I must cease.

A Letter to America

Margaret Atwood

Margaret Atwood (1939–), born in Ottawa, Canada, attended the University of Toronto, Radcliffe, and Harvard. At a young age she decided to become a writer, and she has published a remarkable list of novels, poetry, and essays, along with forays into other genres such as children's stories and television scripts. She is best known, however, for her novels: The Edible Woman *(1969),* Surfacing *(1972),* Lady Oracle *(1976),* Life Before Man *(1979),* Bodily Harm *(1982)* The Handmaid's Tale *(1985),* Cat's Eye *(1989),* The Robber Bride *(1994),* Alias Grace *(1996),* The Blind Assassin *(2000),* Oryx and Crake *(2003), which was shortlisted for the Giller Prize and the Man Booker Prize,* The Penelopiad *(2005), and* The Tent *(2006). In this letter published in the* International Herald Tribune, *Atwood expresses her deep concerns regarding the direction of United States domestic and foreign policy in the first years of the twenty-first century.*

1   Dear America:
          This is a difficult letter to write, because I'm no longer sure who you are.

Some of you may be having the same trouble. I thought I knew you: We'd become well acquainted over the past 55 years. You were the Mickey Mouse and Donald Duck comic books I read in the late 1940s. You were the radio shows—Jack Benny, Our Miss Brooks. You were the music I sang and danced to: the Andrews Sisters, Ella Fitzgerald, the Platters, Elvis. You were a ton of fun.

Reprinted from *The Globe and Mail*, March 28, 2003, by permission of O. W Toad Ltd. © O. W Toad Ltd., 2003. Reprinted with permission of the author.

You wrote some of my favorite books. You created Huckleberry Finn, and Hawkeye, and Beth and Jo in *Little Women*, courageous in their different ways. Later, you were my beloved Thoreau, father of environmentalism, witness to individual conscience; and Walt Whitman, singer of the great Republic; and Emily Dickinson, keeper of the private soul. You were Hammett and Chandler, heroic walkers of mean streets; even later, you were the amazing trio, Hemingway, Fitzgerald, and Faulkner, who traced the dark labyrinths of your hidden heart. You were Sinclair Lewis and Arthur Miller, who, with their own American idealism, went after the sham in you, because they thought you could do better.

5   You were Marlon Brando in *On The Waterfront*, you were   5
Humphrey Bogart in *Key Largo*, you were Lillian Gish in *Night of the Hunter*. You stood up for freedom, honesty and justice; you protected the innocent. I believed most of that. I think you did, too. It seemed true at the time.

You put God on the money, though, even then. You had a way of thinking that the things of Caesar were the same as the things of God: that gave you self-confidence. You have always wanted to be a city upon a hill, a light to all nations, and for a while you were. Give me your tired, your poor, you sang, and for a while you meant it.

We've always been close, you and us. History, that old entangler, has twisted us together since the early 17th century. Some of us used to be you; some of us want to be you; some of you used to be us. You are not only our neighbors: In many cases—mine, for instance—you are also our blood relations, our colleagues, and our personal friends. But although we've had a ringside seat, we've never understood you completely, up here north of the 49th parallel.

We're like Romanized Gauls—look like Romans, dress like Romans, but aren't Romans—peering over the wall at the real Romans. What are they doing? Why? What are they doing now? Why is the haruspex eyeballing the sheep's liver? Why is the soothsayer wholesaling the Bewares?

Perhaps that's been my difficulty in writing you this letter: I'm not sure I know what's really going on. Anyway, you have a huge posse of experienced entrail-sifters who do nothing but analyze your every vein and lobe. What can I tell you about yourself that you don't already know?

10   This might be the reason for my hesitation: embarrassment,   10
brought on by a becoming modesty. But it is more likely to be

embarrassment of another sort. When my grandmother—from a New England background—was confronted with an unsavory topic, she would change the subject and gaze out the window. And that is my own inclination: Mind your own business.

But I'll take the plunge, because your business is no longer merely your business. To paraphrase Marley's Ghost, who figured it out too late, mankind is your business. And vice versa: When the Jolly Green Giant goes on the rampage, many lesser plants and animals get trampled underfoot. As for us, you're our biggest trading partner: We know perfectly well that if you go down the plug-hole, we're going with you. We have every reason to wish you well.

I won't go into the reasons why I think your recent Iraqi adventures have been—taking the long view—an ill-advised tactical error. By the time you read this, Baghdad may or may not look like the craters of the Moon, and many more sheep entrails will have been examined. Let's talk, then, not about what you're doing to other people, but about what you're doing to yourselves.

You're gutting the Constitution. Already your home can be entered without your knowledge or permission, you can be snatched away and incarcerated without cause, your mail can be spied on, your private records searched. Why isn't this a recipe for widespread business theft, political intimidation, and fraud? I know you've been told all this is for your own safety and protection, but think about it for a minute. Anyway, when did you get so scared? You didn't used to be easily frightened.

You're running up a record level of debt. Keep spending at this rate and pretty soon you won't be able to afford any big military adventures. Either that or you'll go the way of the USSR: lots of tanks, but no air conditioning. That will make folks very cross. They'll be even crosser when they can't take a shower because your short-sighted bulldozing of environmental protections has dirtied most of the water and dried up the rest. Then things will get hot and dirty indeed.

You're torching the American economy. How soon before the answer to that will be, not to produce anything yourselves, but to grab stuff other people produce, at gunboat-diplomacy prices? Is the world going to consist of a few megarich King Midases, with the rest being serfs, both inside and outside your country? Will the biggest business sector in the United States be the prison system? Let's hope not.

If you proceed much further down the slippery slope, people around the world will stop admiring the good things about you.

They'll decide that your city upon the hill is a slum and your democracy is a sham, and therefore you have no business trying to impose your sullied vision on them. They'll think you've abandoned the rule of law. They'll think you've fouled your own nest.

The British used to have a myth about King Arthur. He wasn't dead, but sleeping in a cave, it was said; in the country's hour of greatest peril, he would return. You, too, have great spirits of the past you may call upon: men and women of courage, of conscience, of prescience. Summon them now, to stand with you, to inspire you, to defend the best in you. You need them.

<u>Revising Literacy</u>

The Hole in The Wall Project by Sugata Mitra
Nurturing Creativity by Elizabeth Gilbert

Appendix I: Paper Assignments

Lived Literacies: Base Assignment

We began this semester discussing our own and one another's literacy histories, and by looking at the literacy histories of other people. In paper #1, each of you will have the opportunity to create a more formal version of your own literacy history. As our readings have illustrated, there are a number of ways to focus your literacy autobiography: working from a significant event or events, following a chronological pattern, discussing significant people involved in that history, etc. You can choose any one or any combination of these focusing methods or use one that you have seen at work in a literacy autobiography that we have not read together as a class. As you make these decisions, remember that your literacy history should do more than tell a story or strive for self-expression; it must also reflect on the significance of the literacy issues implied by the narrative. This means that you must explore events, people, the chronology of your literacy history or whatever focusing strategies you choose to identify and analyze the larger themes and issues they raise. Reviewing and analyzing information to identify its significance in some larger frame is a common expectation for students in higher education; this assignment will help you meet these expectations in effective ways.

In Paper #1, then, you will reflect upon the different facets of your literacy history and upon your ideas of literacy more generally. Your purpose here is to discover how the reading we have done to date sheds new light on your own literacy history, and to communicate that discovery to others. It is important to remember that you are not only telling a story; you are also reflecting on the significance of your story in relation to the theme of literacy. Like each assignment this semester, your paper must include a visual; for this paper your visual will be a cover page that prepares the audience to enter into your text as an engaged reader.

We will spend a significant amount of time discussing invention, arrangement, and revision activities for this assignment. Due dates appear on your syllabus

Requirements: 3-5 pages in 12 point font; one-inch margins; a cover page with a visual that helps readers enter your paper in the right frame of mind; a short letter explaining your invention, arrangement, and revision choices for this assignments.

Lived Literacies: Base Assignment #2 for International Students

We began this semester discussing our own and one another's literacy histories, and by looking at the literacy histories of other people. We focused specifically on the different assumptions about writing, reading, and researching that we bring with us to this class and how different cultural practices favor different ideas about invention, arrangement, revision, style, and delivery. As our readings have illustrated, there are a number of cultural differences in the ways that people think about reading, writing, and using other voices in their own texts. Understanding and thinking through these differences can help you make successful transitions and meet expectations for reading, writing, and researching that you will face in higher education in America. As we review the invention, arrangement, revision, style, and delivery activities that will help you respond successfully to this assignment, remember that your paper should do more than tell a story or strive for self-expression; it must also reflect on the significance of the differences in the literacy practices you discuss and show how those differences can help undergraduate students be successful in higher education in America. Reviewing and analyzing information to identify its significance in some larger frame is a common expectation for students in higher education; this assignment will help you meet these expectations in effective ways.

In Paper #1, then, you will reflect upon the different facets of your literacy history, upon your ideas of literacy more generally, and upon the differences between and among literacy practices and assumptions in ways that help show how those differences can help undergraduate students be successful writers, readers, and researchers. Your process should shed new light on your own literacy history and on how cultural assumptions and practices inform your literacy history. Your purpose is to use these new insights to help other students in other sections of this course understand some cultural differences in our assumptions about literacy and our literate practices to enhance their chances of success as they pursue undergraduate degrees at MSU. Like each assignment this semester, your paper must include a visual; for this paper your visual will be a cover page that prepares the audience to enter into your text as an engaged reader.

We will spend a significant amount of time discussing invention, arrangement, revision, style, and delivery activities for this assignment. Due dates appear on your syllabus

Requirements: 3-5 pages in 12 point font (not counting the cover page); one-inch margins; a cover page with a visual that helps readers enter your paper in the right frame of mind; a short letter explaining your invention, arrangement, and revision choices for this assignment.

Purpose   Subject

Audience   Self

Lived Literacies: Women's Music in Higher Education

We began this semester discussing our popular music literacies affect how we know what we know, what we know, and how memory creates images and ideas about women in America.

In paper #1, each of you will have the opportunity to explore and communicate some of the ways that your music literacies can help you make the transition to writing in higher education. In paper #1, each of you will explore some aspect of your own popular music literacy history to identify the ways it can be revised and transferred into your life as a writer and/or reader in higher education. Here are some examples of types of literacy you might explore:

- reading music: e.g., understanding things about rhythm, tone, interpretation and performance that can assist you as a writer
- how listening to music everyday and memorizing songs can enhance your academic writing
- how thinking/singing/talking/reading in verse allows for expression of things that don't get expressed in prose and other forms of texts
- exploring how verse forms help you make new connection between in-school and out-of-school writing
- analyzing how the moves and emotions of other popular female songwriters and/or performers help us understand and deal with audience/readers
- explain how knowing more than one genre of popular women's music helps you deal with the various genres of writing you encounter in undergraduate education in America

As our discussions about women's lyrics and music illustrate, there are a number of different ways to focus your paper: working from a significant song(s) or album and it's impact on your writing; tracing certain verse forms and their influences on in-school and/or out-of-school reading and/or writing, exploring popular women in music and their lyrics as a way to understand what it means to build historical context from individual events/lives, etc. You can choose any one or any combination of these focusing methods, use one you discovered outside of our readings, or create your own. As you make these decisions, remember that your music literacy history should do more than tell a story or strive for self-expression. Your purpose is to help others with that type of literacy to engage it successfully as they start their college/university educations. This means that you must explore the connections between that type of literacy meeting literacy expectations in higher education. Understanding the significance of what you learn is a common expectation for students in higher education; this assignment will help trace your learning in effective ways.

Like each assignment this semester, your paper must include a visual; for this paper your visual will be a cover page that prepares the audience to enter into your text as an engaged reader. You will also want to think about the visual and audio representations of songs that you want included in this paper. Remember, this particular assignment calls for an essay in a fairly traditional academic style. You will have opportunities later in the semester to create other kinds of texts.

We will spend a significant amount of time discussing invention, arrangement, revision, style, and delivery activities for this assignment. Due dates and other requirements such as length and form expectations will be discussed in class.

Cultural Literacies Base Assignment

Background: Our study of critical discourse reveals to us that considering familiar things in new ways enhances our understandings of the artifacts that inform our everyday lives. In this paper you will have the opportunity to analyze an artifact or artifacts from popular culture to shed new light on the meanings of those artifacts. Remember as you select your artifact(s) that your goal is to practice using critical analysis and critical writing to generate new knowledge about those artifacts.

Context: In a democracy people are confronted with various images, discourses, points of view, etc. Clearly, democratic consciousness requires us to do more than merely identify with these things. To make decisions about where we stand on political, ethical, commercial, etc. interests, we must use our critical abilities to analyze the artifacts that create and inform our realities. In this paper, your job is to select a set of cultural artifacts that share a common theme and use the critical concepts we have studied to discern what those artifacts mean and how they mean what they mean.

Rhetorical Situation: To help the faculty, staff, and administrators of institutions of higher learning understand the popular cultures that inform the lives of their students, you have been asked to analyze some popular culture artifacts for a column in the *Chronicle of Higher Education*. You have approximately 1500 words to get the job done. MSU students have been selected to submit columns because of their reputation as writers who prose is engaging and in need of little editing; please remember this when you submit your piece for consideration. As with paper #1, you may choose to use invention, arrangement, and revision strategies we have seen at work in our readings and/or some you have created yourself or seen at work in other texts. Some visual representation of your artifacts is required by this assignment.

PASS Analysis:

Purpose

Audience

Subject

Self

Cultural Literacies: Women's Music in Higher Education

Background: Our study of remakes of popular women's music and songs reveals to us the ways that cultural contexts leads to revision of forms and methods of delivery as well as to changes in the interpretations of songs and performances. Considering how contemporary, familiar versions of remakes have historical referents and less well-known cultural associations enhances our understandings of these artifacts as they inform our everyday lives. In this paper you will have the opportunity to analyze an artifact or artifacts from women's popular culture music to shed new light on the meanings of those artifacts. Remember as you select your artifact(s) that your goal is to practice using critical analysis and critical writing to generate new knowledge.

Context: In a democracy people are confronted with various images, discourses, points of view, etc. Clearly, democratic consciousness requires us to do more than merely identify with these things. To make decisions about where we stand on political, ethical, commercial, etc. interests, we must use our critical abilities to analyze the artifacts that create and inform our realities. In this paper, your job is to select a set of artifacts from popular women's music and use the critical concepts we have studied to discern what those artifacts mean and how they mean what they mean.

Rhetorical Situation: To help the faculty, staff, and administrators of institutions of higher education understand the popular cultures that inform the lives of their students, you have been asked to analyze some popular women's music for a column in the *Chronicle of Higher Education*. Ultimately, your discussion should help the readers see how popular culture might enhance student's lives in higher education. You have approximately 1500 words to get the job done. MSU students have been selected to submit columns because of their reputation as writers who prose is engaging and in need of little editing; please remember this when you submit your piece for consideration. As with paper #1, you may choose to use invention, arrangement, and revision strategies we have seen at work in our readings and/or some you have created yourself or seen at work in other texts. Some visual representation of your artifacts is required by this assignment. It must occur within and enhance the text itself.

PASS Analysis:

Purpose

Audience

Subject

Self

Disciplinary Literacy Base

Background: The first two formal paper assignments for this course gave you opportunities to identify themes and terms for analysis so that you could begin to understand and practice meeting the expectations for writing in higher education. Paper three allows you to continue practicing sound analytic and critical thinking, reading, and writing skills while also introducing you to the ways that research and participating in important academic discussions further prepare you to use literacy in effective ways.

Requirements: Different academic disciplines have different ways of presenting and analyzing information, different ways of building knowledge, and different ways of presenting knowledge in written forms. This paper gives you the opportunity to begin building your own understanding of how writing is created and operates within a discipline of interest to you. You may choose what ever discipline you wish to examine for this project. Whichever you choose, you must engage in at least the following activities:

Analysis of one textbook from that discipline
Analysis of at least one scholarly article from that discipline
Analysis of at least one interview you hold with a professor from that discipline

Your paper must be 6-8 pages long, in 12-point font, with one-inch margins.

Writing Context: Many students come to higher education with only a vague idea of what it means to become a participating member of an academic discipline. Your purpose in this essay is to give students who are new to the academic discipline you have chosen to explore an introduction to the expectations for writers in that discipline. Ultimately, your paper should help your audience understand the ways that writing is used to create and communicate knowledge in ways that help them become better readers and writers within the discipline under discussion.

Base Remix Assignment

PROJECT #4

- For this project you will transform one of your essays into an alternative form. You might choose to create a video, a photo essay, a PowerPoint presentation, a web page, a painting, a brochure, a poster, a basket, jewelry, etc. Please bring all of your essays to class on _____ so that we can start discussing how we might select essays and alternative forms of presentation.

Your final project should be accompanied by a memo that explains:

- the SWAP elements of your project
- why you selected the essay and alternative presentational form(s) that you chose for this project
- Your process (RAIDS) for creating the project
- How your process helped you improve in areas listed on the shared learning outcomes for Tier I Writing grid that accompanies your syllabus

We will create an evaluation guide for this project together in class.

Note: SWAP refers to Subject, Writer, Audience, Purpose
RAIDS refers to Revision, Arrangement, Invention, Delivery, Style

Remix for Women and Music in Higher Education: Cross-Class Assignment

Our classes have been exploring the ways that gendered forms of literacy affect our ideas about ourselves, others, and how we know what we know. In this project we will focus on identifying and remixing male assumptions about college women and female assumption about college men. You will all have a lot to say about what the final project from your class will look like. Dr. DeJoy's class will write a song and produce a video; Mr. Craig's class will write and produce an iMovie. But to get started we will engage in the following process:

Each class will identify the major assumptions the group holds about members in the other group.
Those assumptions will be delivered to the group under discussion.
The group under discussion will then create a remix from those assumptions.
The remix will be delivered back to the group who provided the assumptions.

In other words, Dr. DeJoy's class will identify assumptions about college men to Mr. Craig's class; Mr. Craig's class will deliver assumptions about college women to Dr. DeJoy's class and so on.

The objective of this assignment is for you to take what you have learned about writing in multiple genres and creating a new approach to communicating effectively using multimodal strategies.

Each class will also create a group reflection about the project in which they discuss what worked well, what should be done differently when Dr. DeJoy and Mr. Craig do the project again with their classes next semester, and how invention, arrangement, and revision were used to create the remix product. We hope that we can all get together to view the final projects, but our schedules may make this difficult.

Here's the proposed schedule for our work

November 9/10: classes create the list of assumptions for the other class
November 11/12: classes look at the assumptions from the other group and make decisions about the remix product that they will produce and begin work on remix project
November 16/17: work on remix project
November 23/24: finish work on projects
November 25: Dr. DeJoy's class project due

Final Assignment Base

Learning Outcomes for Final Papers: This assignment asks you to reread the papers and projects that you (and, perhaps, your peers) have created this semester to meet the following major goals:

- Use writing for purposes of reflection, action, and participation in academic inquiry
- Engage in reading for the purposes of reflection, critical analysis, decision-making, and inquiry
- Read in ways that improve writing, especially by demonstrating an ability to analyze invention, arrangement and revision strategies at work in a variety of texts
- Exercise a flexible repertoire of invention, arrangement, and revision strategies
- Demonstrate an understanding of research as epistemic and recursive processes that arise from and respond back to various communities

This does not mean that other style and delivery issues are not important. But they should be made in relation to the elements of PASS you define for your paper and will be evaluated in the larger frame of the project.

Requirements for this Assignment:
Your final paper for this course gives you the opportunity to revisit and revise your literacy history for a specific purpose of your choosing. For example, you might choose to revisit and revise your literacy history to clarify how your writing, reading, and researching practice have changed this semester and how you will apply them and/or continue to develop them in the future. Or, you might decide to revisit and revise for the purpose of helping in-coming students understand the big picture of Tier I

Writing to enhance their chances of success in the course. We have seen many writers use themes to explore their lives as literate human beings. Alternatively, you might decide to use this paper opportunity to explore and explain how what you have learned this semester will be applied to some form of non-academic writing that you have become interested in (e.g., songwriting). The important thing to remember as you use Purpose, Audience, Subject, and Self to define your final project is that the final product should help you both 1) revise your individual literacy autobiography in a significant way by drawing on course materials and activities and 2) create strong points of significance.

Your final paper must be submitted with a cover letter explaining:

1. which invention, arrangement, and revision strategies you used and why
2. which purpose, audience, subject, and self you chose for the assignment and why.

You should be prepared to discuss your chosen theme in class next week.

This paper should be 7-9 pages long; it counts for 30% of your final course grade.
Your visual(s) can be placed anywhere; it will be evaluated for effectiveness in relation to your points of significance.

Due dates appear on your syllabus.

Base for Women and Music in Higher Education

Your final paper for this course gives you the opportunity to use a literacy theme to revisit and revise your literacy history. We have seen many writers use themes to explore their lives as literate human beings. The important thing to remember as you choose a theme is that the theme should help you both 1) revise your individual literacy autobiography in a significant way by drawing on course materials and activities and 2) create strong points of significance.

Your final paper must be submitted with a cover letter explaining:

1. which invention, arrangement, and revision strategies you used and why
2. which purpose, audience, subject, and self you chose for the assignment and why.

You should be prepared to discuss your chosen theme in class next week.

This paper should be 7-9 pages long; it counts for 30% of your final course grade.
Your visual can be placed anywhere; it will be evaluated for its effectiveness in relation to your paper and will be given a separate grade. That grade will go toward the oral presentation portion of your course grade.

Due dates appear on your syllabus.